HE'S NOT GOING TO CALL

HOW TO GET OVER IT, START DATING AND FIND A GOOD MAN

ROMY MILLER

HE'S NOT GOING TO CALL

HOW TO GET OVER IT, START DATING AND FIND A GOOD MAN

ARTRUM MEDIA

For those who do not wait in vain.

Paperback ISBN-13: 978-1-938107-52-8
Paperback ISBN-10: 1-938107-52-7

Published by Artrum Media.

eBook ISBN–13: 978-1-938107-53-5
eBook ISBN–10: 1-938107-53-5

CONTENTS

CONTENTS

BE SAFE

Before we begin, I want to briefly touch on a subject that's quite important; and that is safety. I like to try and mention this in all of my books because it is rather important. And it's important that you *keep yourself safe.* I think it's obligatory to include a warning about some of the men you might run across. And I don't mean for this to be a downer, but we have to be safe in these days and times. We're women and we know there are a lot of creeps out there, unfortunately, and some of them want to hurt women. So, this goes without saying, but I will say it anyway: Be safe. Be aware. Be cautious. Always tell someone where you are going and with whom. Always listen to your gut, as it will let you know if something is wrong with certain men.

Got it? Good.

An Introduction

Without going into too much detail about how all this is going to work out, I wanted to introduce this book by saying this: Men should start treating women with more respect. There, I said it and when I say it, I mean, they need to do what they are genetically predisposed to do and that means they need to be the ones who do the calling.

While that's all good and well, the problem is they don't do this, do they? And this drives us bonkers. I mean, ahem…crazy. Anyway, when this happens we begin to feel the need to call him or text him or whatever. And this is supposed to be okay nowadays, right? Women supposedly *can* call men and do all the things that have traditionally been assigned to the man in the relationship. However, while this should be the case, it just doesn't work in real life because when you do break this rule, nothing good usually comes of it. It can make a girl look and feel bad, like she's doing something that she shouldn't. No one wants to feel like a pest and no one likes it when someone ignores them. And this is where feelings of desperation come in. Most times, feeling desperate to talk to him or to get him to text you back gets in the way of good, common sense. You *have* to know what's going on, right? You have to know why he hasn't called, right? It's understandable. And that's when you call or text and that can, inevitably, lead to him ignoring you. And then you end up feeling worse than you did before.

But what if you could stop this pattern of desperation right in its tracks? But more importantly, what if you didn't have to worry about if a guy calls or if he doesn't? And what if there was a way for you to take more personal responsibility in the matter? What I mean by this, is that when a woman goes after a man who isn't that interested, she tends to make a fool out of herself. And I say "fool" for want of a better word. However, what she doesn't realize is that when she has to do this for a man, he just isn't worth her time. This means that you can go ahead and mark him off your list without succumbing to calling and wondering if he really likes you or not. You're taking measures to clear out the men who are ambivalent and also taking measures to find yourself a good man, one who will, quite possibly, be better for you in the end.

Doesn't that sound good? Would it not be great if you could be the girl he wants to call? You can. You can do that. And it doesn't take that much, just a little self-awareness and the ability to beat him at his waiting game.

And this is what this guide is about. It's about figuring why he's not calling, how to not call *him* back, and, more importantly, how to get him to call *you*. Yes, that's a bit dizzying, but the point is quite simple: You want men to call you and you don't want to chase after them. You want it the other way around, right? Well, if that's what you're after, you've come to the right place.

I'll give tips on how to get men interested and keep them interested, as well as the other topics mentioned above. More importantly, I will touch on subjects about becoming more self-aware and getting past the temptation to succumb to desperate measures, therefore getting over potentially making a fool of yourself. It's about being cognizant of what you are doing and how to stop doing it so you don't end up getting embarrassed or feeling humiliated. Those aren't very good feelings to feel, are they?

But, in the end, it's all up to you to stop being desperate. It's up to you to get over it, start dating and find a good man. We're going to keep things simple and to the point as I am not a fan of minutiae. What we want to accomplish is getting past the BS that makes us feel bad about ourselves and onto the real, good stuff like finding a good man and, perhaps, even having fun while dating. What a concept, right?

To boil it down to the essentials: In this book, I will tell you how to land the man of your dreams using the old standby of being confident while using techniques that are sure to drive him crazy. In a good way, of course.

Ready for the challenge? Let's get to it.

THE URGE TO CALL

We've all done it. It's like we can't help ourselves. It's there, our phone, staring at us, urging us to pick it up, call and… Well, see what happens. It is the urge to call.

Do you find yourself in this predicament more than you'd like to admit? You liked a guy but then he didn't call. It's happened to the best of us. But let's pause and examine this a little more closely. Let's just take it a step at a time. Let's as they say, break it down. Okay? First comes the date. Right? It went well, you had fun, blah, blah, blah. He dropped you off or you two parted ways at the restaurant and then you went home with the warm fuzzies. You might have even had a nice dream about you and him on some tropical island. You could see yourself with a guy like that. You liked him and you can't wait to hear his voice again, like tomorrow, first thing. But if he wants to call later, that's okay too.

But then something odd happens. It's like… The sound of silence. Crickets. You phone isn't blowing up. It's not ringing. No, it's as quiet as a mouse. You feel just a little puzzled and then you begin to get the feeling that maybe he isn't going to call. Or maybe you don't. Maybe you still think he *is* going to call and so you wait. For a while and then it just becomes too damned much, and so you start calling or even texting him.

First it's just to make sure he's still alive, right? I mean, accidents do happen. Just that initial call to make contact. That's all. To let him know you're still interested. He needs to know you're interested, right? You don't want him to think you didn't like him, right? He certainly won't call if he thinks this.

So, you make the call and he doesn't answer. It goes into voicemail or whatever. Maybe you text him and get the same result. Fine. You made the effort and now you'll just wait for him to return your call. So you wait. And wait.

Then comes the silence. Nothing's happening. He's still not calling back. Does your phone need charging? Check it. No, its fine. Then you start going back and forth with yourself, asking yourself why he's not calling. Then you start tearing yourself down, thinking it's all your fault. In an effort to not completely kill your self-esteem, you turn your attention to him. Then you call him again. Over and over again. Then you start wondering what's wrong with you. Did he not like you? Did your hair look weird? Did you eat too much at dinner? Maybe you talked too much? And why isn't he picking up when you call? Why isn't he replying to your texts? He did, in fact, give you his number, didn't he? If so, why isn't he responding?

And on and on until you, almost quite literally, want to pull your hair out. This is called obsessing and it's not the most fun place to be. It makes you feel a little bad about yourself, doesn't it? At this point, it's time to face the truth.

Are you ready to hear this? It might be tough. It's gonna be hard. Okay, let's just do it. Let's pull it off like a bandage and feel the sting. Let's just go ahead and get this out of the way. Ready? He's not answering because he's not interested. In effect, he's ignoring you. And, boy does that smart.

As I said, it's happened to the best of us.

After that first date when he doesn't call or text, it seems as though we are helpless to do anything about it other than just wait by the phone or call him. We start to make nuisances out of ourselves. We start to act *not* like ourselves. We cease being the intelligent women we are just because some jerk gave us his number then decided to... Well, he decided to reject us.

Hate that. Hate that a lot.

What to do? What to do? Part of us wants to get a hold of him and just... Well, not do nice things. We're past that. How could he do this? It's humiliating! Why was he nice in the first place? You just don't get it. Is there something wrong with you?

Okay. Stop. S-T-O-P. Yes, stop everything and ask yourself what the heck you are doing. You have to stop because if you don't you might risk going certifiable.

No. There is nothing wrong with you. You've just found yourself in the obsessive loop. That's all. It's that loop a girl finds herself in sometimes with she meets what she perceives is a good guy then realizes he doesn't like her. Then she starts obsessing and making a fool out of herself. It doesn't stop there. Some girls even go beyond calling. They start stalking the guy. They start showing up at their rejecter's houses or apartments or even jobs. It gets that bad. But it doesn't have to. In fact, you don't ever have to put yourself in this situation again. And how can you avoid it? By doing three little things.

Ready?

To avoid finding yourself in the obsessive loop:
- Face the truth and the truth is that he's not going to call.
- Refuse to give in to the obsessive loop and you do that by refusing to call or text him at all.
- Accept the fact that he didn't call and that he's not going to.

You have to realize that facing the truth isn't a bad thing. It's quite a good thing because it can keep you from ending up with egg on your face. Who wants to be known as a pest? And, really, that's what you become when you can't give up on a guy. But if you can learn to let go and chill out, as well as learn a few tricks of getting his attention, you can be the girl he does want to call. You can actually turn it around on him and have him start calling you obsessively. Wait. Maybe not obsessively but regularly.

You have to realize that you have the power. You can take control. But first, you have to be willing to accept that he's not going to call. Don't obsess about it. And you have to be willing to be the one who takes a chance to let a guy be the one to call. And, also, you have to be willing to admit that he's not worth it if he doesn't call. That means you have to be willing to let it go and move on. It's really that simple.

Let's step to this.

WHAT THE HECK AM I DOING?

Before we go any further, let's address something. As women, we sometimes find ourselves wanting to call men who haven't called us. But that isn't really the issue. The issue is why do we feel the need to do this when we know, more often than not, it won't turn out well. Why do we feel this desperation?

I believe it's because many of us have some need to control the situation. That's all. We want to be in charge. It's in our nature. We're not all wallflowers. And, I believe, this is the way Mother Nature intended it. I mean, if we waited on men to do the things we need them to do, we'd be waiting a long time. And nothing would ever get done, right?

And we also start losing our senses. If we could just take a step back and a deep breath we would see the situation for what it is. And it's only us going on a date and liking a guy who doesn't really like us back. That's all. And it's getting past that hurt and humiliation to get onto another guy who will love us the way we need to be loved.

Want to know the irony? The irony is this: If you can keep from calling him, he might just call you. No, it won't be on your terms and it might be weeks, possibly even months after you've gone out and forgotten about him. It might not be ever. But if you can refrain from calling and obsessing about him, then your chances of him calling you have risen substantially.

You take control back by letting it go. That's right. Be willing to let go of the control in this situation. Be willing to take a step back, a deep breath and let whatever will be, be. It's not that hard to do when you get right down to it, either. It's simply refraining from calling.

Yes, you do run the risk of him not calling. Is that really that big of a deal? Big whoop. There are a ton of single men in this world and I am more than sure a few of them are actually willing to call a girl within a reasonable amount of time. I am sure there are many of them who want to call and be nice. Not all men are jerks. They're just not. Not all men are running from what they perceive as an out-of-control situation. Not all men want to make a girl wait on a call.

So, it then becomes a situation of simply weeding out these guys—the ones who don't call—from the ones who will. It's a process of elimination, that's all. There are good men out there and it's up to you to find the one who will not only call but will be good to you once he does.

I look at it like this: You're the woman; therefore he's supposed to call you. That's the natural order of things. He's the man so let him do the work. I know it's hard. We want to know, right? We want to know if this thing is going to go somewhere and, more importantly, we want to be able to steer it in the direction we most desire. However, it's not that simple. It's just not. We have to be willing to let him call us. That's all. We have to be willing to take that chance. And all we have to do to take it is simply let go. Sounds simple enough, doesn't it?

What Happens When You Call

In my opinion, I don't see anything wrong with calling a guy. You like him; he supposedly likes you, right? Where's the problem? Where does it all go wrong? Why does it all go wrong? It goes wrong because we, as women, want to be able to make a relationship happen. We want, as I have already said, control. And it's hard to wait, isn't it? The clock is always ticking. But that's the way it is. It just is. Be willing to accept it as such and be willing to let go of the control and allow the man to do his job.

Yes, we wonder why he's not calling. And, yes, there are a plethora of options to choose from. Maybe he didn't like you. *Ouch*. Maybe he was just bored. That can hurt, a lot. But it can only hurt if you let it. This is why you have to let it go. It just looks bad when a woman chases after a guy who doesn't want her. And, yes, that seems harsh. But that's the truth and, as we all know, the truth can hurt. But if you can get past that and look at it from a different perspective, you can save yourself quite a lot of hassle. The point is to accept that it didn't work out and stop caring why he didn't want you and move on. Once you can do that, you can release yourself from this vortex of pain and potential embarrassment and move on.

And that's what gets most of us. We get embarrassed, humiliated when he doesn't call. We wonder what's wrong with us. This is just wrong. Don't do this to yourself. There is nothing wrong with you just because some jerk didn't call. This is why you shouldn't allow yourself to go down this road. You deserve better than that.

I have always said this: If they don't want me, then I don't want them. Yes, it's a hard-nosed approach but it's also says a lot about self-respect. Besides, why would you want to be with someone who doesn't want to be with you? In the end, all this will do is cause you pain and, as I said, possible embarrassment. Who wants that? Who wants to look back and feel the sting of humiliation from acting like a fool over a guy who doesn't want to be with you? Not me and more than likely not you. But if you can stop the cycle before it gets started, then you can overcome this and move forward. It's getting stuck here, waiting on a man to call, that seems to cause a lot of problems, but if you can somehow remove yourself from the situation, then you can get past the pain and onto something that might just be better for you in the long run.

Yes, perhaps you think this guy is the man of your dreams. Yes, you probably "connected" with him and had a great time. Now this is where everything goes wrong. And that's because he's obviously turned you down. You can't figure out why, either. And now he's planted himself into your head and you can't get him out. Now comes the important step and that step entails you accepting the situation for what it is and that he's not going to call you and for you to keep yourself from calling or texting him to "check in" or whatever. It entails you avoiding "finding out" why he didn't call. It involves you moving on and saying to hell with him and his stupid games.

But what happens if you do call, if you do take that step? Well, if it all turns out well, he's happy to hear from you and asks you on a date. This could happen and it has happened. But is it worth the risk? Especially when all signs point to the contrary? Because, if you call and he's not interested in you, more than likely he will ignore your call which could, quite possibly, spur you into calling or texting him even more. And then it just all goes to hell from there.

But let's take a moment and look at it from his perspective. He might just think of you as a nice girl he didn't really connect with. And then, when you call, he feels bad because he doesn't want to answer. And so, the dance continues. You get obsessed, he gets annoyed. That's what usually happens when you call. And it's not pretty.

Right now all you can do is take the hint and move on. You have to find something to do that doesn't involve this guy. Otherwise, you end up looking... Well, terrible. Desperate even. Who wants that? No one! No one wants to look like the needy girl who's begging for attention. It's unseemly, isn't it? But all you have to do is stop this behavior before it reaches fever pitch.

And, obviously, you don't want to find yourself outside of his house or waiting for him after work. You don't want to call him and then hang up, either. And, if you go to the places that you know he'll be... Come on, girl, you're better than that. Much, much better.

Keep in mind that these situations are extreme but they do happen. Maybe it's the whole mindset of thinking that if they "see" you, then they'll remember how good you were and want you. But most likely he's not going to come around and suddenly remember how great your conversation was if you randomly show up at his work or at the bar he frequents or whatever. He's going to get worried that he might just have someone who's a little crazy. You don't want to be that girl, believe me. That's why it's imperative that you just let him go. Leave him alone. And make a point to never do this again or, better yet, don't start in the first place.

Obsessing over a man for whatever reason—you had a good date, he was an unrequited crush or whatever—is a sure-fire way to not only make yourself feel like an obsessive maniac but to look like one, too. That's why you have to do whatever it is you have to do to get this dude out of your mind.

Keep in mind that he's a man and is not without flaws. Even if you managed to land him, you might end up seeing him for who he really is. And that might disappoint. (It's happened to others, believe me.) You have to get over the idea that it was meant to be. If he didn't want you, he didn't want you and take it as a sign that it would not have worked out anyway. And there could be many reasons why it didn't but you'll never know because if you do these things like incessant calling or texting, he will think you're a little nutty.

You don't want that, do you? Then don't do these things. Have more self-respect than that! You're a smart, beautiful woman. Act like one. He's the one who's supposed to chase you, not the other way around.

Love, like so many other things in life, can hurt. And, boy, can it suck, too. It's when we're rejected that we go a little nuts. It's when we can't get past wanting someone who doesn't want us that we feel really bad about ourselves and that's why we *have* to have them love us. But it rarely works out like that. Step back and take a deep breath. It's time to move on from all of this and onto something much, much better.

Keep in mind that this bit of information can be used as a powerful relationship screening tool. If he doesn't call or even text you, it's not going to work out. This way, you don't waste a ton of time or effort on him and you can move onto someone better without any much embarrassment.

THE MARRIAGE ISSUE

I just wanted to touch on this briefly. It's the point of not making marriage your goal when you're first getting to know a new guy.

Yes, marriage is kind of the point of dating. I know this and you do, too. But if you push it in a guy's face too soon, he's more than likely going to hightail it out of there. Men do want to get married; they just don't want to be *pressured* into getting married. And, if they start feeling *pressured*, they get scared and want to run and hide. Pressuring anyone into doing anything is a surefire way of getting them not to do something. It's really true. You don't like to be pressured, do you? No. Probably not. And most other people in the universe don't either.

This isn't to say that you're doing this. You might not be. It might be as simple as you two didn't click on your date or whatever. And that's fine. Not all relationships succeed. Some just fizzle out before they even get started. That's life. It's not that big of a deal in the bigger scheme of things. You just have to look at it from a realistic perspective.

But, back to the subject at hand. It's never a good idea to thrust the subject of marriage, i.e. long-term, heavy commitment, in a man's face from the get-go. Even if he's digging you and you can tell he's digging you. Even if you're getting the vibe that he could be "the one" and you want to be his "one." You have to keep in mind that it almost has to be their idea. If you can understand this, then you can understand why it might seem like a big deal to most men. And, let's face facts; no one wants to feel pressured into doing anything, like I've said. That's life. We don't want anyone telling us what to do. And, for men, once they tie the knot, that's usually what their wives do, isn't it? It is. They tell them what to do most of the time. That's reality. That's the way it works. So, from this perspective, you can kind of see where this dude might be coming from.

Marriage is a big commitment and therefore, it can be a big issue. Men see it as such because once they're married, they are going to assume a lot of responsibility. Yes, you will too, but if you know anything about men, you'll realize that they look at things differently. So, don't just assume they're all running scared because they just want to play the field more or whatever. This could be a reason but another reason could be that, well, they're scared and, if you if you look at it from his side, you might see why he gets a little uneasy about the topic. To many women, it's a beautiful white dress and eventually cute babies. To men, it means putting in more hours at the office and giving up a lot of freedom. Marriage can be tough and perhaps many men see it more realistically than women. They know that once they're in, they're all in. Therefore, they want to be sure they're marrying the right woman.

So, can you see why he might be afraid at first of this? I thought so. Why not give a guy a break and give yourself a break too? Marriage is a good goal, but it's not worth losing a good guy over just because you want him to know how much and how soon you want to get married. Just have fun at first and enjoy his company. You have to let things evolve naturally. That's what dating is supposed to be about.

I think this is the main reason guys get scared when they first go out on a date with a girl. Keep in mind that when you go out, it's best to curtail certain subjects just because they're heavy and don't really make for a fun, casual encounter. Dates are just that—dates. They're meant to be something people do in order to get to know each other better. They're really just a way a guy and a girl can get together, share a meal or a coffee and learn a little something about one another. If it goes beyond that, it goes beyond that. If it doesn't, fine. It doesn't.

Why is this, though? Why would this subject of marriage make a guy want to run like the wind? Like I said, you have to look at it from his perspective: You've just met. You don't know each other that well. You're already talking marriage. Understand what I'm saying? He just thought you were going out to see if you might want to date more. He's there to meet someone new. That's probably how he's looking at it.

Now, how do you look at it? If you look at it like you're just going to see if this dude could be the one to put a ring on your finger, you're looking at it all wrong. If you go into it with this idea, it's more than likely not going to work out. Sure, there are some men out there who are ready to get to it and get married immediately. But even those men want to get to know a woman better than a stranger before they pull the trigger.

I understand that as we get older, we do get a little desperate to get married and have babies. This is normal and it's natural. There is nothing wrong with it. However, you can't really let the guy you're going out with know you're into this as much as you are. If you do, you can come off as seeming a little desperate. And men, like everyone else in the world, can smell desperation. You don't want this. You want to have fun. You want to see if you like this guy and then move on in the appropriate direction. Right?

So, it's important to make a first date just that—a first date. Get to know him and have fun. Enjoy your food or drink or coffee or whatever. And then move on.

As long as you don't mention marriage or babies, it should be fine. I say let him be the one to do the mentioning. Let him bring this subject up. If he brings it up on the first date, just smile and tell him sure, you want that too…someday. Never act like you're ready to elope at a moment's notice. This will let him know you're a woman who's not desperate to get married and this will let him know you're one worth seeing again.

WERE YOU WRONG ABOUT HIM?

We all know how easy it is to get hung up on a guy but, at the same time, be completely wrong about him.

When we like someone a whole bunch, we want them to like us back and sometimes we tell ourselves little white lies to get through the day. However, this just leads to pain and suffering. Being honest with yourself is a one-way ticket out of misery. And all you have to do is admit that, maybe, just maybe, you were wrong about this guy. He's not the one and he ain't gonna be. That way, everyone leaves the situation without feeling overly hurt and hoarding unpleasant feelings.

Yes, it would be good if a guy would just say how he really feels, wouldn't it? If he would just let us know that he doesn't want to date us. Yes, it would hurt but there is a certain freedom in that, isn't there? It's like he's letting us off the hook. But, usually, men don't do this and I believe they don't do this in order to spare our feelings and keep us from blowing up at them. Maybe there are other reasons, too, but those two are the ones I am most aware of.

But even if he doesn't come through with some good, old fashioned honesty, you still have to own your own feelings and emotions. Yes, you liked him and he didn't like you back. That sucks. It really does. But you have to realize that sometimes emotions can lead us astray and we get wrapped up into believing in something that, simply, wasn't there. Like thinking some guy likes us when he really didn't. And that makes us wonder if we were wrong about this guy all along. Sometimes, yes, we were.

If we could all get to this point, then none of us would have to go through the misery of trying to figure out if someone likes us or not. But it doesn't happen that often. People aren't that honest with their emotions and they're not that honest because they don't want to risk hurting someone's feelings. This get messy real quick. Also, most people don't like confrontation. It's human nature. And that's where the trouble comes in. And that's why it's just easier for him to ignore your calls. It's not that hard to figure out. What's hard is accepting that this is what's going on and moving forward from it.

Keep in mind that it is very important not to make him the end of be all of your existence. He's just a man. That's all. He's probably not even a rock star or a billionaire playboy. So, with that in mind, is he really worth all this fuss? Ask yourself you that. Is he? Is this man worth you making a fool of yourself over? Step back, mull it over and find your answer. It's more than likely going to be a resounding "no," isn't it? More than likely.

However, in order to move on from this, let's figure out what might just have scared him away in the first place so that, perhaps, none of this happens again. Ready? It's in the next chapter.

WHAT MIGHT HAVE SCARED HIM AWAY

Let's just get straight to the point of this chapter and the point is to attempt to define what could have scared this man away. Did you do something wrong? Just what was it that made him run in the other direction? What happened? Was it as simple as you two, simply, didn't click? Or was it something else? There are a lot of reasons why, but you have to realize that you might not ever know why. And we all know not knowing why is something that drives us crazy. And that's what makes us want to call him and find out.

It's a good idea to stop yourself before this happens. (We've already discussed this.) However, let's turn to the issue at hand and that issue is this: What happened that might have scared him away?

Let's just break it down. First of all, you have to keep in mind that going on a date is for men, as it is for women, simply an opportunity to see if the other person is relationship material and, possibly later on, marriage material. If you don't feel that initial spark, why would you continue on with it? It won't do either of you any good. And if he isn't feeling it, he's going to cut his losses.

But why can't he just tell you he isn't interested? Well, should he have to? Think about it.

Here's where common sense kicks in: You have to be responsible for your own feelings. You can't wear them on your sleeve and hope everyone takes care of them. This isn't to say you must hide your feelings for a guy; it's just to say you can't lay it all out on the table and hope against hope that he treats them with kid gloves, i.e. kindness and consideration.

Because of this, on a date, we make the assumption that just because we like a guy that he automatically likes us and when he doesn't call, we begin to wonder what scared him away. We begin to question ourselves: Was I too talkative? Not talkative enough? What was it? This leads to a lot of self-doubt and soon we doubt we'll ever be able to date again.

But it doesn't have to be like that. If you just step back and see the situation for what it is you can begin to get over it. And, let's face facts, it was just a date that didn't go as well as you had thought. And just because you liked him, doesn't mean he liked you. There is a possibility that you misread the situation. Why think of it as some big deal? Isn't it better that you know early on rather than wasting time on a relationship that is doomed to fail?

The key here is acceptance. Accept that sometimes things don't work out and be willing to be okay with that. This can be hard but if you can do it, you might just find that it makes your life a whole lot easier.

However, now let's talk about the possibility that the two of you really hit it off and you were sure that things were going great but you're still waiting for him to call or text. Did you do something that scared him away? Maybe and maybe not. Maybe you did, but maybe it really was due to his own issues. Maybe he perceived things the wrong away. Maybe you were too good to be true. Perhaps he even got scared because you were *too* nice. Maybe you just didn't click. That's right. Have you ever thought of that? You two might not have clicked. That's all. He just wasn't feeling it, as they say. Sometimes, it's just that simple. Sometimes it's just that obvious. No need to make a big deal out of it.

But I think the main reason men lose interest and don't call is because you have triggered something in them that scares them. And this thing is a fear of commitment. If you're too enthusiastic about a guy and too nice and too good to be true, he's probably going to start to feel a little uneasy, a little suspicious. He might even start thinking that you want him so much that you can't see straight and, inevitably, you will try to pin him down and get something out of him he might not be ready and willing to do at this stage in his life. In essence: He might just think you want to get married. To him. Like, yesterday.

That probably wasn't even what you were after, but he's got it all confused now. It's like he's thinking that you're going to try and make him do something he isn't ready to do. So, what probably scared him was looking down the barrel of a big commitment. That's all. Whatever you "did" caused him to back away hurriedly. And all you might have done was casually mention someone's engagement ring or said you wanted to get married someday or whatever. Maybe the fact that you were so good and so nice brought out his insecurities. And if this is all it took to scare him away, let him stay away. He's obviously got some problems you don't want to deal with.

However, it is important to see it from his viewpoint as well. Just like women, men have to decide if they want to be in a relationship or not. Some men are more than ready to jump in immediately. Others, not so much. That's where you came in. You were really nice on the date. You, perhaps, looked a little eager. He got scared that you might want him to "do something." That something is getting him into a committed relationship. And so he backed away. And then you started calling, which scared him even more. He wasn't quite ready for this, or didn't know he wasn't ready and when you did what you did, he realized this. And now he's, in effect, hiding.

Sounds ridiculous but that's what he's doing. He's gone into hiding to avoid getting into a relationship because he's probably afraid of getting married. Things were going faster than he could handle. He wasn't ready for a commitment. He just, simply, wasn't ready to jump in with both feet.

Here's the caveat: Even though we get a bad rap for it, men change their minds maybe even more rapidly than women. Just because you gave him a little scare doesn't mean he's not interested. However, if you call him over and over again, he's going to retreat into his shell like a turtle and never be heard from again.

But here's the thing: All you have to do now is not call him. You have to let him do the legwork from here on out. He has to be the one who calls. He has to be! The problem, I think, was that he perceived that you were doing the deciding for him about getting in a relationship and he didn't like this. Well, who would, really? No one wants to be backed into a corner. Here's a good analogy: It's like when you're walking through the mall and those people at the kiosks want you to try their products and try to force you into coming over and getting some lotion or perfume or whatever. Has that ever happened to you? I am sure it has. And what do you do? If you're like most humans, you do whatever it is you have to do to avoid going over there. You don't want to get over there and be forced into buying something you didn't even know you wanted in the first place. Right? Right. Maybe this is the way he feels, too. He doesn't want to be forced into getting into something he wasn't sure he wanted in the first place. So, if you look at it like this, you might see where you went wrong. Be willing to take some responsibility for it. Be willing to get over it, too.

The gist is this: He doesn't want to be told or even forced into a relationship. It has to evolve naturally. And, really, it should.

So, all you have to do is give him breathing room. Let him decide if he wants it or not. And you just sit back and relax. If he wants it, fine. If he doesn't, okay. You'll be cool either way. In the end, no one wants to be with someone who doesn't really want to be with them. It's that simple. And no one wants to be backed into a corner and forced into doing something they didn't decide on their own to do.

It's important to keep this in mind whenever you venture out on a date. No matter how well you think it goes, giving him a call afterwards might push him over the edge into scaredy-ville. This is why it is so important to just hold back and let him acclimate. That way, if you did say or do something that gave him a scare then he makes the decision to move forward or not. It's in his hands what to do. It's up to him. Let him make the decision. What choice do you really have? You can't force someone into a relationship just as you can't force someone to like you.

Leaving it in his hands puts you in a better position, too. You don't have to call and, inevitably, look like you're begging to be his girlfriend. All you have to do is answer the phone if and when he calls. And then it's your call, quite literally, which direction to take with this guy.

A Matter of Communication

What if the guy in question was a person you were seeing on a fairly regular basis? What if you and your guy actually had a relationship of sorts? Perhaps, even an intimate one? What if you thought the two of you had something going on and he just all of a sudden stopped calling? It's like one day you two were hitting it off and the next, all you got was radio silence. What happened? What went wrong? Did he die or something? Hopefully not. Most likely, no. He just stopped calling. And that makes a very peculiar situation for a girl to be in.

Again, you have to break it down to the basics. You have to figure out why he's all of a sudden out of the picture when you thought you two had a future together, when you thought you had something special, something worth pursuing, something worth your time and energy. And one of the main reasons might just be that there was a breakdown in communication.

Yes, indeed, this might simply be a matter of communication, or, rather, miscommunication. If you're seeing a guy and he stops calling or texting or dropping by your place or whatever, then it might be that something happened to scare him off. And it might not be anything to do with you, not necessarily. It might just be he thought you had *this* sort of relationship and you thought you had *that* sort of relationship. What I mean by this is that maybe he thought it was more fun and less serious and you thought it was fun but getting serious or vice versa. Perhaps you thought it was more meaningful than he did. Perhaps you thought it was leading somewhere more serious and he just wanted to keep it casual. Perhaps he wasn't ready to go all in and bailed before you hooked him.

Men can be creatures of habit and once some of them establish a routine, they like to stay in it. However, if "something happens" to dissuade them off their path, they can and will bail without word. Yes, in a lot of ways, it's a coward's way out. Commitment can scare a man. And if he thought you were just "having fun" and got the idea that you were more into him than he was into you, he might have left just to avoid any sort of emotional blowup.

The idea here is to be sure that you two are on the same page. This is why it's always a good idea to establish boundaries. It's good to lay it out on the table and let him know what you expect, or at the very least, what this relationship means to you. And, if you think about it, maybe *you* were the one giving off the vibe that what you two had together didn't mean that much. That you were just having fun. This might have been what made him change his mind and leave. Remember, it can work both ways and that's why it's important to be cognizant of what you're putting out there.

I suppose my advice here would be to really be aware of what you say and how you act when you get involved with a guy. Know that if you give off the impression that you're just in it for the fun times, then that's probably what he's going to think, too. Many times, men think in black and white terms. What you lay out on the table is most likely what he's going to take from the relationship. If it's all just laid back and causal, like you're friends with benefits or whatever, that's what he's going to think. Sure, he might want more but he might think you *don't* want more. Get what I'm saying? The fault, usually, can't always lie entirely with him. You have to take responsibility for the way you act and how people perceive you.

This is why it's so important to become more self-aware. What you give out to the world is what the world usually perceives you as being. Most times, people aren't going to take the time to go through the motions of trying to figure you out. It's your job to help them.

One way to avoid this in the future is know what you want out of a guy and out of a relationship. Maybe you started this thing thinking it would just be fun but fell for him over time. That's cool. But it might be helpful that you clue him in on how you're feeling earlier on. I'm not saying to come out with an "I love you! Let's get married!" a month or so after you've met him. But what I am saying is to check him out and see how he's feeling. If he's as into you as you are him, cool. But if he's not, and you can usually tell if he's not, then it's time to either have a talk or to break ties. Why prolong the inevitable? To just drag something out that's not going anywhere is almost torture because, in the end, it will get harder and harder to get out of. Or, he might just take off without another word.

So, check him and see where he stands. You shouldn't be afraid of scaring a guy off especially if you've been seeing him for a while. You have to start being honest with your feelings and, I believe, he should start being honest with his, as well. If you think a relationship is something it's not, then both parties need to verbalize this and move on or, possibly, even change the relationship. When it comes to this, both of you are responsible for where it's headed. At this point, you're in it together.

So, therefore, if he's really digging you, you'll know that. If he treats you like his girlfriend, you'll know that too. But if he's just calling up for a booty call or whatever, you know he's probably just using you. And, let's be honest, men love sex. And once they find a woman with whom they can do such things with little or no strings attached, they're probably going to take full advantage. If you're just in it for the sex, too, then fine, but let him know this too. But if you're not, then he might need to be told where you stand. No one likes to be used and no one likes to feel used. If you're feeling this way, then this guy might not be worth the trouble you're putting into him. Take stock and see how you really feel about the situation and then take the appropriate action. If it's to stop seeing him, then good. If it's to have a talk and see if he's interested in taking it to the next level, cool. If it means all you can do is just be friends, okay, fine. But do something and don't feel bad about yourself in the meanwhile.

It's all a matter of communication. Being upfront and honest can be your biggest asset. If you're willing to lay it all on the table a little earlier on, you might just avoid this happening. And if he flies off? Then you're better off, right? Let him go and keep in mind that next time, playing it a little differently might produce different results.

GET PAST THE REJECTION AND GIVE YOURSELF A PASS

This is a very important step. Sure, it sucks when someone hurts your feelings but you have to keep in mind that if you get hung up on it, it could taint your future relationships and could impair your self-esteem. Who wants to be the girl that feels like she's unwanted? No one. And the guy who did the rejecting? Well, obviously, he wasn't that nice. This is why it's important that you get past the rejection of him not calling.

But it's hard *not* to get hung up on rejection. It's even harder to admit that we were rejected. Who wants that? No one I know. However, I think the basis of this is that we fear being humiliated and we resist admitting that we've been humiliated. That stings, doesn't it? It stings because we put ourselves out there to be loved and someone, some guy, rejected that. It can make a girl feel very bad about herself.

What can you do to not get hung up on this? What can you do to get past it? You have to first admit it to yourself that this has, in fact, happened. Yes, you've been rejected. Admit it. Accept it. It's a hard thing to do but it's an important step. It's hard to do because, as I said, it is humiliating. But if you leave it undone, it's just going to become the elephant in the room. And when that happens, things can get a little miserable until you finally deal with it. So, it's best to just be upfront and honest with yourself about what really happened and also to accept what happened. That's what matters now. Without this step, you might get hung up and not get back out there and start dating again.

Most importantly, the key is to *not* focus on rejection. Yes, acknowledge it, obviously. But then don't focus on it. Don't make it your reason for being, i.e. you're the girl he didn't want. Don't put that label on yourself. It's unfair and unkind to yourself to do that. And it will more than likely hinder you from finding a better man. Just because one guy didn't want you doesn't mean there aren't many others out there who will. Tap into that because that, right there, is self-confident behavior at its best and right now this is probably what you need most. Don't continue to feel inferior and belittled and humiliated. If you do, accept these feeling but move on from them. Don't let them keep you hung up on feeling bad about yourself. Don't get stuck in this moment. This is one guy. One guy! He's not worth all this trouble.

So give yourself a pass on this and get past the rejection. That's about the only way I know to get past it. Sure, you do need to accept it and then deal with your feelings that emerge from it. And once you do that, don't focus on it. Don't look at the date you went on as a complete failure. Don't look at the guy who didn't call as someone who set out to hurt you because, for all you know, he didn't. Just look at these things as something you did once or someone you liked for a while. This is just something that happened in your past and decide to leave it there. Accept that it didn't work out and then move forward. Don't make the rejection from some guy into a life changing moment. He isn't worth it.

Next, it's important to let go. Yes, you feel humiliated, perhaps even like a fool but it's essential that you just let it go.

Letting go is simply accepting what has happened. It's also verbalizing your feelings about it. Talk to a trusted friend or relative about it and listen to what they have to say. If you don't have anyone to talk to, write it down. The thing is to get it all out and let go of the feelings you have about what has happened.

After you do this, you need to start with a clean slate. Wipe all this mess away and vow to get back out there and start dating again. If you get hung up on this issue and feel overwhelmed by it, all that will do is hold you back from experiencing better dating experiences, and, maybe, even better men.

If you can get past the rejection, you can move forward. Yes, it can be hard but it's doable. So, do it and move onwards and upwards. It's better than wallowing in self-doubt, isn't it?

So, I say, have your moment. You might be feeling anger and that's okay. Who wouldn't? That's fine. Whatever you are feeling is fine. So take a few minutes to feel what you need to feel but then make a point to move past it, get over it and not get hung up.

CONFIDENCE IS KEY

The best way to get a guy interested in you is to have confidence. Yes, everyone knows this but it does seem to be forgotten from time to time.

Confidence is mostly about attitude. It's all in the way you carry yourself, so if you think of yourself as being a confident person, that's how you will present yourself to the world, i.e. *I am confident and I can do as well, if not better, than most.* Confident people know who they are, are proud of where they come from and don't let others get them down. When something happens to them, they have their moment then pick themselves right back up and move on. That's being confident.

Therefore, if you think of yourself as being a confident person, that is to say, secure in yourself, this is the image you present to the world. And the world usually responds well to confident people. The world likes confident people. I mean, what's not to like? Most confident people have a good attitude and don't bring others down. They're actually fun to be around.

Keep in mind that women who are self-confident are women who attract men like crazy. Men really dig these women because they are easier to interact with and carry on a conversation with.

But what if you don't have that needed confidence? What if you have issues with this or that that bring you down? You just have to work on those issues, whatever they may be. Just take a few minutes every day to sort through them but don't let them hold you back. Sure, some guy might have broken your heart and made you feel bad about yourself. This happens. Just feel your feelings and move on. That's what being a confident person is about.

To be more confident in relationships, just start thinking of yourself as a woman guys make a big deal over. *He likes me because I'm worth liking.* Guys are more than willing to spend time with women they feel *have it going on.* And all you have to do in order to "have it going on" is be nice but be willing to hold back a little and act only slightly interested in him.

Also, be approachable. Don't be standoffish. Men approach women who they feel won't reject them. So, be relaxed and confident in yourself and see where it takes you.

Some women, on the other hand, are really aggressive. If this is you, keep in mind that it can scare guys off. All you have to do is be aware of what you are doing and just tone it down a little. Men want to think that they're in charge, so be willing to allow him to be in charge. Or, at least let him think he is.

Another thing to keep in mind is simply going with the flow. Confident people do this. If a guy wants to stop by at a bar and talk to you, then that's cool. If he doesn't, that's okay, too. Confident people are freer in their thinking and don't get hung up on this one guy talking to them because they know there are a lot of guys out there who are willing to take the time. Getting hung up on just one guy is never a good idea.

Along with this is the attitude of just not caring so much about people liking you. The less you seem to care about some guy, the more he seems to care about you. It sounds so counterintuitive but it's true. This is allowing the situation to be what it is without trying to control it. This is being confident. This can so work to your advantage if you use it right. And all you have to do is sit back, relax and act like you just don't care. You don't care if he talks to you or calls you or whatever. And if you don't care, chances are, he might just. And that's what you're after. You want him to be the one calling and making the dates.

Sure, when you meet someone—or see them from across the room—throw him a smile and let him know it's okay to approach. Just don't start fall all over him when he shows up. Just say "hi" and let him take it from there. Let him do the work. But go easy on him and respond to what he's saying without taking over the conversation. This is being a confident woman, someone who is willing to hold back and see where things go.

As you're talking, see if you're holding his attention. If not, get up and excuse yourself. Never be hesitant to pull the plug when you know this thing isn't going anywhere. If you can do this, and do it with confidence, you'll show him that you don't have to have anyone's undivided attention to survive. More than likely, this will spark his interest even more and he'll want to know what's up with you. However, he might just bail altogether and if you're confident, that's okay with you. It was a risk worth taking. Remember, nothing ventured, nothing gained.

And if you have to do it, if you have to leave the situation for whatever reason, don't beat yourself up later over it. Don't say to yourself, "If I'd just stayed and talked…" No. You have to be willing to walk away, otherwise you might find yourself wanting to hold his attention and doing something stupid in order to do so. It's about not being desperate. It's about getting over it and moving on. That's being confident.

Men love a challenge, so be a challenge to them. Make them work for it. You've got what he wants so it shouldn't be any other way. You're a woman and you're confident and if he can't be bothered, he's not worth it.

Men love a woman who keeps them guessing. They want us to be a mystery. If we go in and *try* to get him to like us, we're no longer a mystery. We're the needy girl who wants a date from them and God knows what else. If you're confident, you don't need anything from this guy. You're cool. You know he should be working to charm you, not the other way around.

The gist is this: Be confident in who you are and be willing to walk away. You're more than worth a guy making a fuss over. Start thinking of yourself as such and soon you shall be.

Focus on What You Want

One way to move forward and get over the jerk who didn't call is to focus on what you want. But first you have to figure out what this is. What do you want? Do you want to start dating again or do you want to take some time for yourself? Whatever you decide, go for it. It never hurts to take a step back and figure out where you want to go and what you want to do.

If you want to move forward with finding a new guy right now, focus on what you want out of a relationship. Figure out the kind of guy you'd like to date next. Decide the best way to meet him. Make a plan, too. It's not hard to meet men, but meeting a good one can be tricky. That's why you have to know yourself very well and know what you're willing to put up with and what you won't put up with. Figure out your own likes and dislikes.

In order to have a good, solid relationship, people have to have commonalities. They have to be like-minded. For instance, maybe you're into rock and roll but you always meet men who love country and western music. On the surface this might not be a deal breaker, but having this distinct difference in tastes in music can be an indicator of other differences. That's why it's important to find a man who mostly likes what you like. Yes, polar opposites do attract but they can clash, too and cause a lot of problems. So, keep that in mind.

What if you don't know what you want? Perhaps you've just been floating around, hooking up with men here and there just because they fell into your life or whatever. Maybe you don't know what kind of man you'd like to meet because you've only met random guys that you never seem to connect with on a deeper, more intellectual basis. If this is true, then take a step back and reevaluate things. Reevaluate what you want from a man and out of a relationship and vow to find that. If you're more of cerebral girl, find a guy like yourself who's into rocket science or whatever. This is finding commonalities and they can be crucial in establishing a lasting bond. I mean, you have to have something in common with your man or you'll just bore one another to death. If he loves video games and you like going to museums, it might not work for very long. And then you have to go through the trouble of breaking up and then… Well, you get the point.

Keep in mind, though, that it's perfectly okay to like someone who has different interests. He just has to *not be opposed* to your interests. If he likes video games and you like museums, he can't be opposed to you going to museums while he stays home with his video games. It's about finding balance, a yin for your yang, so to speak, and this is a cool way to go about it. So, when you two meet up again, you'll enjoy each other's company that much more. This is a great way opposites can get along.

It's very important to define what you want out of life. It's important to know what you want. If you don't, you're sort of just out there, floating around and bumping into whatever guy comes your way and doing whatever you have to do in order to get by. However, you can turn this around by simply being aware that, yes, you do have choices in the matter and the choices start when you take the effort to figure out what you want.

So, one of the best ways to figure out what you want is to take the time to sit down and write it down. If you have to marinate on this for a few days before actually sitting down, then do so. But it is imperative that you take the time to define what you want out of life, out of a man, out of a relationship. If you just want to date and have fun, then that's cool. But if you want to get married soon and start having children, that's fine as well. And then you have to find like-minded men that will enable you to do these things. Obviously, you're probably not going to find a man who's marriage material at club. But you might find him at the company picnic. See what I'm saying?

Therefore, the next step is just to figure out what you want and then go for it. Figure out where you might meet your new man and then go meet him. It can be that easy. So, don't make things overly complicated. Keep it light and airy and just be willing to find someone that you want to be with, that will love you for who you are, that will take part in your hobbies or at least allow you to do them without giving you a hard time about it. Opening yourself up to all the possibilities can be extremely daunting but you have to do it. I mean, you have to get out there and be willing to try and find something great.

Be willing to go with the flow and just get out there and be open to new possibilities. That's all you really have to do. If you really and truly know what you want, you can usually figure out a way to get it.

Focus on what you want and then let go of what you don't. It's really that simple.

SELF-DOUBT FOR NICE GIRLS

This is a hard thing to swallow but it warrants mentioning. So, let's do it.

There are some women out there who really want certain guys to like them. When they find one, they become really, really nice. In other words, they try to win him over, so, they want to show this guy how nice they can be to him. And so they shower him with affection and maybe even gifts. If he screws up by not calling or ignoring them, even though they are hurt by it, they just shrug it off and smile. They're nice, you see. But nice can, more often than not, turn you into a doormat.

Here's the rub: If you do really, super nice things for a guy you like, you might see it just as being, well, nice. But he might not. He will more than likely see it as a little desperate and wonder why you're being like this. He might even wonder if there is something wrong with you. In turn, he might start ignoring you or even avoiding you so he won't have to go through the pain of hurting your feelings or, even worse, a bad break up. If he's not that nice himself, he might even start seeing just what he can get away with.

So what do you do? Turn into a raving lunatic who yells and screams if she doesn't get what she wants? Or keep being a super nice girl who gets walked all over? Is that all the choices you have? I think, for many women, they think it is. You can either be the mean girl he's scared to cross or the nice girl he pushes around.

It doesn't have to be like this. Not at all. Not ever. Take a breath and listen. Being the nice girl isn't the same as going overboard and allowing someone do as they please while you stand by with a smile. You can be nice without being awful. It's a fine line but if you want a man to treat you better, you'll have to learn to walk it.

Being too nice might just be the reason men don't call back and the reason he avoids you. It might be the reason he wants to break up. And he can do as he pleases because you haven't set any boundaries and you've allowed him to treat you this way. You teach people how to treat you which means, if you let them, they'll treat you any damned way they want to. By this I mean, how you let them treat you is how they will treat you. Guys are bad about this. But, on the other hand, in a way, I think they *want* to be told what to do and how to treat a girl. Maybe they're just all clueless about women or something so this is why I say that most of them treat us in the way we *teach* them to treat us. And if we act like it's okay if he does what he wants and forgets to call or whatever, then he's going to keep doing it. Men are creatures of habit. "Well, you didn't *say* to call," he might tell you with a dumb look on his face. It's like they can't figure out that, hey, this isn't appropriate behavior. They're just going on what you're giving them. That's all.

I'm not saying all men are like this but a lot of them are. "But she didn't tell me she wanted something for her birthday." Ugh! Of course, you want something for your birthday. Everyone wants a present on their birthday. That's the way it works. But if you have to work for it and scream about it, what good is it? You want him to just do it on his own, right? Well, good luck with that. Men don't operate like this. Sure, you might see some handsome man on the TV doing things like this but it's probably because he's got some coach in the background instructing him.

That's reality. It can suck. That's just the way it is sometimes.

So, what happens if a guy does something like this to you? What can you do? You can tell him about it. You don't have to yell, but you do need to say something about it. You can say, "I didn't expect much but I thought you'd do a little something for my birthday." That's it. Put the guilt screws to him. I mean, what kind of jerk doesn't remember a girl's birthday? But what if this makes him break up with you? Then bye-bye birdie. Who wants a man who can't do something as simple as picking up a gift and gets angry when you say something about it? Do you? Ask yourself that. Is that the kind of man you want? One who has to be poked and prodded to do anything?

And what kind of guy just acts like he can do whatever he wants and get away with it? The guy who's with a girl who's got too much self-doubt and can't assert herself, that's who. It's that simple. He will try and get away with anything he can if he isn't told that this isn't appropriate. And if you're always allowing this to happen without ever calling him out on his BS, then that's probably how this thing will go from here on out. Unless they already know how, men have to be taught how to treat you. And if you can't tell him, then he's going to take the easy route out and do as he damn well pleases.

And here's the caveat: He wouldn't be treating you like crap if you had never allowed it. If you hadn't been so nice. If you had stood up and demanded better treatment. But how do you do that? You just do it! If he hurts your feelings or crosses a line, then you call him out on it. You have to do this or he'll just keep being bad. It's really that simple. Will he get any better if you do it? Who knows? But at least you told him how you felt and I'd be willing to bet that felt pretty good, didn't it? Well, there you go. If he flies, then the next guy will be that much easier because you can start off with asserting yourself and not being his doormat. And from there, it might just be smooth sailing. Who knows? The possibilities are endless.

This is why communication is so important. If you never let him know how you feel, then he won't know how you feel. And if he doesn't know, then he'll never be able to do better by you. You have to let him know so he can treat you well. It's that simple.

The bigger question might be why do you think you have to be so nice? Why do you? I think women who feel they have to be so nice just simply have a lot of self-doubt, and, let's be honest, dealing with men can lead to this. Men can make any sane woman go bonkers from time to time. Yet, perhaps, this self-doubt is rooted in another issue. Maybe it comes from a different place. Maybe it has something to do with your childhood or a past relationship or whatever. If so, take time to figure out why you feel the need be so nice and let people walk all over you. And then, stop doing it. No one deserves to be treated badly, especially if they treat others so nicely. But it happens. So, learn to deal with it and learn to be more assertive. All you have to do in order to be more assertive is to just open your mouth and let a guy know how what he does makes you feel. And you don't have to yell and scream about it. I am certainly not saying to turn into a full-throttle crazy person. No. I'm saying be nice but don't over-ingratiate yourself. Don't go that extra mile for him at least not until you're in a relationship. Make him work for you. You deserve it. Don't shower him with gifts, either. He's supposed to be giving you stuff, especially at the beginning, to win your love. If he can't do that, he's not much of a prize, if you ask me.

Dealing with men and their issues about calling or not calling can make a normal girl crazy and with good reason. It can also lead to self-doubt and lowered self-esteem and, if you already possess these character traits, this can make things even more difficult. You might think, "I was so nice and he didn't call! Why?!" And, obviously, this leads to even more self-doubt. You might start wondering what's wrong with you and all that nonsense.

Keep in mind, there's nothing wrong with you. You're just being too nice to these guys. Men, I don't believe, really want a woman they can push over. They really don't like this. Instead, they want someone who isn't afraid to stand up to them and hold their ground. This shows them they have a strong woman and a strong woman is a valuable asset. She is someone worth knowing and, more importantly, keeping. They want someone on their level who challenges them. Men want a woman, not a wimp. Just like women want a man, a real man, not someone they can push around and badger without him ever speaking up to defend himself.

Get what I'm saying? Men like challenges. If you're too nice, you don't present much of a challenge. And, like I said, you don't have to go all bitch-queen on him. Be cool and confident. Set your boundaries. Know what you're willing to put up with and what you're not willing to put up with. And be more assertive. You have to ask for respect or, more than likely, you won't get it.

All you have to do is start holding back a little and stop giving so much. That's all. Give him just enough to keep him interested. Once you do that, he will see you're not a pushover and that should entice him to want to get to know you better. And to not treat you badly.

Self-doubt isn't nice for anyone, especially not girls. Being nice and being a pushover are two totally different things. Being willing to stand up for yourself is one of the greatest gifts you can give yourself. So, give it to yourself.

'Nuff said.

TAKE BACK YOUR POWER

Your power as a woman comes from the idea that you're potentially unattainable. It's that you're a mystery. It's in the allure of just being a woman. That's why guys love women; that's why they run after us. We're something they want but can't always get. At least not right away and definitely not without trying.

But if you start making all the moves, he may start holding back. If you do the calling or chasing or whatever, he's probably going to start ignoring you. And then it just goes to hell from there. You are no longer a mystery to him. You're an open book, a story that's telling itself, perhaps a little too quickly. You're revealing too much of the plot and making yourself into a person he wants to avoid. Perhaps even a person who is showing her desperation. And, boy, does that suck.

I believe all of this could be avoided if women would just take a breath and take their power back, the power we all have that has been granted to us just by the fact that we are women. We're *supposed* to be a mystery to men. We're *supposed* to be potentially unattainable. We're supposed to be alluring. We're supposed to be a challenge. We're supposed to hold back and let him try and figure out how to woo us. It's part of the screening process of nature. He has to prove himself of being a good mate. Being these things sparks interest. This makes them want us. But, if we start playing our hand too soon, they disappear into the abyss, never to be heard from again.

It's easy to do. Taking your power back is very, very easy. So, how do you do this? How do you take back your power? Simply stop waiting for him to call or text. Also, don't call him. Ditto on the text. Reclaim your power. It's yours for the taking.

So, keep in mind that if you do the pursuing, the guy you're pursuing probably will see it as if you are pushing him into doing something he doesn't want to do. And then he withdraws and nothing can get through to him. He doesn't want to be badgered and he doesn't want to be told what to do. (At least not yet. That can happen later if you get into a relationship with him.) In those first few, crucial days following a date or just an introduction, it's imperative that you hold back and let him make his mind up about what to do. Sure, this is surrendering control, but you can't push for something he might not be willing to give. Remember this is the way it's supposed to work. He either calls or he doesn't. If he doesn't, move on to the next one. And be willing to move on to the next one. Allow yourself to *feel* and then *free* yourself of this failed relationship, even if it never actually materialized. If you've acted desperate and it backfired, as it usually does, then be willing to admit that and just let this one go. It's not worth pushing for if it's been this much trouble from the start.

When you push, you're giving up all your power. When you call him, you're letting him know he's in control. And he's not, not really. Women are usually the driving forces behind relationships. If it weren't for women, most might not exist. However, at first, let him be in control, or at least think he is. Let him take the lead and then see where it leads you. Why not? What do you have to lose? Sure, you could call him and it might be cool. In most cases, this just seems to not be the case. I, personally, wish it were easier. I wish a girl and a guy could just get together just because they want someone to be with and to have fun with and all that good, good stuff. But people, mostly men, like to play games and these games can really hurt a girl.

However, it's just not that easy. If it were that easy there would be fewer miserable people on earth. And so, the dance continues. Nothing we can do about it but try and take our power back. And what do we have to lose? A call or a text from a guy? That's a risk many would be willing to take. How about you?

THE SEX ISSUE

Yes, let's just jump right in on this. Why not? I wanted to get this one out of the way because dealing with the sex issue can be tricky. And it might have been the reason your man didn't call or even text. Yes, it's true. And, yes, this can so suck. If you have sex with a man too early on, he's gotten what he wants and off he goes. That can sting but it's happened more than any of us would like to admit.

So, when it comes to the sex issue, it's imperative to know when to give it up. How soon? In my opinion, it doesn't matter. However, it *will* matter to him. If you give it up too soon, he'll have what he wants and he might just fly like a bird right out of your life. Men see women as conquests and, until you can lay that groundwork of him falling for you, it might be a good idea to refrain from sex. If he sees you as an easy conquest, the challenge of "getting you" won't keep him interested long enough to get to know the actual you. He's already got you so he's most likely finished trying to figure anything else out about you. Therefore, if he can't get to know you, he probably won't fall in love. And he certainly won't call.

Yes, we could lament about how so very wrong this is, but why waste time? Why not just accept the fact that men can be weird when it comes to this subject? And we all know if they get sex too early on, it can potentially ruin a relationship. Why is this? Who knows? Perhaps Mother Nature in her infinite wisdom put this in men's brains to keep the genes spread out or something. I don't know why it is. All I know is that it is a thing and it should be addressed, but not worried over.

I do believe that it is true that if you're overly sexual in the first stages of a relationship, most men tend to back away. That's why it's important to wait a while before jumping in the sack. (At least if you want something more from this guy other than a good time.) If you want an actual relationship, give it time to develop and leave sex out of it for a while. Sex can bring out some awkwardness that otherwise might not have ever surfaced. Keep in mind that you don't have to have sex immediately. Just do it on your own terms, when you feel ready to do it. Also keep in mind that when it comes to sex, later is usually better than sooner if and when you're trying to lay the groundwork of a relationship.

You should be in control of when the two of you have sex. It is entirely up to you, even if he tries to convince you it isn't. This is one situation where you do have all the power. Because you can get pregnant, you are taking on a risk. (Also, be aware of sexually transmitted diseases, etc. It's up to you to be responsible in this regard.) And keep in mind that the longer you make him wait, the more he will appreciate it when it actually happens.

So, when do you do it? I think it's better to make him wait at least a few dates. I don't really like to put a number on this because it varies for different people, so it's best that you come up with a number you are comfortable with. If he's only in it for the sex, at least get a few good dates out of him. If he bails once you do the deed, then he was going to bail all along. And that means he's probably not worth having.

SOMETHING MIGHT HAVE HAPPENED

In the greater scheme of things, something might have happened to your guy who didn't call. It's true that stuff does, indeed, happen. And so sometimes, after you've written him off, he might call or even text you weeks or even months later after your initial date and asks you out. Obviously, at first, you're shocked. Or maybe even confused. *Who was this guy?* Maybe you forgot all about him. If so, do you want to date someone you can't even remember? It's your call but if he's that unmemorable, he might not be the best guy to make memories with.

However, you might want to know why he didn't call in the first place but of course, you can't come out and just ask him. Well, you could. Why not? But more than likely, most women won't ask what happened and then this issue becomes the elephant in the room, hovering heavily in the corner.

But what could have happened? Well, there's a ton of things, really. I mean, the dog *could* have eaten his homework—or his phone. Maybe an ex-girlfriend showed up and got under his skin again. Maybe he fell into a hole of some sort. Maybe he got the once in a lifetime opportunity to date a supermodel, who, subsequently, dumped him.

Maybe he *was* in an accident. I mean, you never know. Life does happen. But maybe the real reason was because he didn't think the two of you were compatible. That's what might have happened and, yes, it's the most obvious explanation. And it's usually the best excuse to move on.

But, what if you don't want to move on from him? What if you want to go out with him again? What's wrong with that? In my opinion, nothing. There's nothing wrong with it. You just have to decide if he's worth pursuing but more importantly, you have to decide if you need to know what happened to make him not call you in the first place. Can you let it go? Does it matter anymore? Does it really matter what he was doing or why he didn't call? I don't think so unless he was drafting a peace treaty for the world or ending famine.

But whatever. The choice to go out with this dude is in your hands. Nevertheless, be aware that if he made you wait this long, it might be that he's not worth the wait. However, if you're still interested, make sure he understands that you are not a person to be taken for granted. Because you're not.

So, do you want to give this dude a second chance? Can you forgive and forget? If you're still into him, why not? He could turn out to be a great guy. You never know. We all make mistakes and we all take things for granted in our lives that we shouldn't. It's called human nature for a reason.

But how to do this? How to handle this delicate situation? I mean, you've come so far and don't want to screw it up now. You know how to handle men better than ever. So, what do you do in a situation like this?

My advice would be this: Make him wait. That's right. When he calls out of the blue, make him wait on you. See if he's really serious this time. Tell him you're busy with work, family, etc. Tell him whatever you feel like and, truth be known, you probably are busy with these things. Make him realize that he might have blown it with you. Make him realize that he screwed up. I mean, he's calling out of the blue, right? The point is, you can't really give him the impression that you've been sitting around waiting on him to call, like you don't have a life or something. If you're too over-eager here, you're probably going to find yourself back at square one. So, just act like you really didn't care that he called, like it was so inconsequential that you almost had forgotten about him. If you want, pretend that you don't remember him at first. Why not? He didn't remember to call you, did he?

Regardless, if he wants a date, tell him you're busy and to call you back in a few days. If he comes through and actually calls again, I'd say he's in. If not, he never was and you just called him on his bluff and saved yourself a bunch of trouble.

And here's the last thing we need to discuss. What if you go out with him again after all of this and he doesn't call again? Then you know what to do, don't you? There's no need to give him a third chance and, of course, there's no need to call him.

MEN ARE NOT SHOES

Yes, I said that. And, yes, I know that sounds like a crazy title for a chapter, but I've got a point I'd like to make. Here goes...

Most women, if not all women, are always on the hunt for the perfect pair of shoes. We have to find *the ones* and once we do that, we have do whatever it takes to possess them even if it's to the detriment of our finances. We get hung up on them and we can't live without them. We obsess over them and once we get them, we're in love. Well, at least until a new pair comes along that grabs our attention.

That's not really a problem, unless, of course, you're going broke from buying too many shoes. The problem comes in when we start treating men like this. Men aren't shoes. Men can't be bought and they can't really be possessed. Well, I suppose some could, but you probably wouldn't want those kinds of men. Even so, the point is that you can't treat a man like a lust-worthy pair of shoes. And what do I mean by this? I mean, you can't hunt him down and buy him. You can't pull out all the stops and hound him and make him love you. You can't shower him with gifts and affection and expect him to do so in return. You can't, in effect, be overbearing. Being overbearing means you run the risk of smothering him and that will make him feel hemmed in and we all know men love their freedom. At least until they get into a relationship.

And why can't you? Why can't you do these things? I mean, you're just showing these guys how much you like them, right? What's so wrong with that? What's wrong is that men don't operate like that. They think if a girl's coming on too strong and being too nice and going out of her way too often, it might be because no one else wanted her. It might mean that she's desperate.

The thing is, I understand completely why women do this. Maybe we think: *If I show him how much I like him, he'll like me back.* Not so much. I don't believe you can ever show your cards to guy, especially in the beginning. I don't believe that you can fall all over him and have him falling for you. I just don't think it works that way. At least not from my personal experiences.

The point is this: If you like him, you have to be willing to take a hands-off approach at first. You have to be willing to let him do the calling and all that. You have to let him treat *you* like something that he really likes and wants, not the other way around. Never let on like he's someone you can't live without. For all you know, you *can* live without him.

You can never go overboard with a man. Never. If you lay it on too thick, he might think you're too good to be true and wonder what's up with you. Hold back and retain your air of mystery. Oh, and wear those new shoes. There's nothing like a great pair of heels, is there? No. And there's nothing like making a man want to get to know you better, either.

LOVE AT FIRST SIGHT?

One reason we tend to get hung up on certain guys is that we all believe in "love at first sight" and we want that to happen for us. Believe me, I've had fairy tale dreams myself. And, yes, I have a hard time admitting this. But I also know the reality of the situation and that is getting to know one another and having common interests is a much better way to start a relationship. That way, you ease into it and you fall in love because you get to know this person better as time goes along. In essence, you fall in love with the person and not in love with love.

Love at first sight seems perfectly doable, too. Why not? Why can't a girl meet the man of her dreams and fall in love just like that? Well, there's a good reason for this and it's probably because it's completely unrealistic.

Yes, there is this thing called reality and it always swoops in to screw things up, doesn't it? The reality is that yes, love at first sight does probably exist, though I've never met anyone who has actually experienced it. And the reality is that, yes, love at first sight is an oh, so wonderful idea. Just the thought of it is enough to turn an ordinary girl into a hopeless romantic. But this doesn't happen often enough to warrant even a statistic about it. That is, if someone actually kept a record of stuff like this.

However, we've all seen the movies where this happens. And this might be one reason we want it for ourselves. Why not? It's so romantic. It's the perfect scenario. You meet, you immediately fall in love, he sweeps you off your feet and maybe, even, to Paris. You have a fabulous wedding and move into the perfect place and…

Oh, who am I kidding? We all know that after the trip to Paris and after the movie ended, things got a little difficult. And that's because reality stepped in. You have to keep in mind that relationships can be tough. And none of them are perfect. However, if we start with the idea of love at first sight and it gets embedded into our heads, we might feel that anything less isn't as good. Like, we ended up with our guy and he wasn't that romantic and it wasn't that romantic how we met him. Over time, this could lead to resentment and all that other nasty stuff no one really wants to think about when they're thinking about love.

Let's be serious. Don't you think it's a little naïve to think a guy is *the one* from the moment you see him? It creates an urgency that could make you end up looking foolish. If it's love at first sight, then, of course, you're going to be willing to do whatever it takes to obtain it. But what if it's not love at first sight *for him*? Oh, boy. We all know where that can lead.

And now that leads us to him not calling. I think when guys don't call girls, girls can get the idea that it was love at first sight because they begin obsessing about him and they create the aforementioned urgency about having him. *You have to have him.* Right? Am I right? I think the reason why is because we start to believe that he's the one and all we're really feeling is borderline humiliation and we want him to call so we can stop feeling so badly about ourselves. And then you add these romantic notions to the mix which further complicates things. This is why it is so important for you to see things as they are and to be more self-aware. You have to know how you're feeling so you don't trip up as often.

However, the reality of the situation is that if it's love at first sight for both of you, he will call you because he won't be able to live without you. And if you feel like this for him and he doesn't feel the same way, then you end up feeling like you *must* connect with him in order to get him on board with how you feel. You think that if you can somehow get through to him, he will start to recognize what you perceive to be his true feelings for you. But he won't. He has to do that on his own. You can't force it on him and you can't make his mind up for him. This is up to him. More importantly, you have to be willing to accept what he does and not get too upset over it if it doesn't turn out in your favor.

The thing is, love at first sight has to work both ways or it doesn't work at all. If you feel it and he doesn't, then it wasn't love at first sight. That's why, when you're waiting on a guy to call, you should *wait* for him to call and not call him. And if he doesn't call? Well, we've covered that.

Keep in mind that love at first sight is a great concept but it just doesn't translate to reality that well. From my experiences, the best relationships start off as friendships. From there, they move on to romantic. After that the relationships can evolve into marriage and then children may follow. In that order, usually, too. Yes, the idea of love at first sight is a great concept but one better suited for a romantic comedy than actual reality.

STOP CHASING HIM AND LET HIM CHASE YOU

In the animal kingdom, the males of the species are the natural aggressors. This means, they chase their females. And they also fight with the males over the females. This means they want the female to know that they have chosen her as a mate and that she is worth fighting over. And sometimes, the males actually get killed in this pursuit of the female. Come to think of it, the animal kingdom is more than a little scary.

But, in a way, it's like this in the human world, too. Maybe without all the fighting and killing. However, men do like to chase but with one caveat, they want to chase the "right" woman. And, obviously, they don't really want to be chased themselves. Some may say they do, or even expect it. But most? I don't think so. It's, in a way, against their nature to be chased. Therefore, it's never a good idea to chase after a man, even if he's a rock star. Why? Mostly because this gets you no respect. That's why. It might be a hard thing to hear, but it's true.

Think about it. Don't you think there is something inherently suspicious when someone becomes overly interested in us? We all do this. We all think, *What is wrong with this person that they are so taken with me? What did I do? Why are they doing this?* It's like it sparks something in the animal part of our brain. We think something is wrong and our defenses go up.

Most times it's just simple infatuation. That's all. And perhaps a little obsession. When we like someone, we *like* them and we want to spend time with them. However, if we become too over-eager and start chasing them, they start dodging us. In other words, just like in the animal kingdom, your prey becomes aware that you are hunting them and they scurry away like a wild animal. In a way, they become too wary to catch. So, you're left empty-handed and feeling a little hungry.

Keep in mind that it's your job to make the man chase you, to make him interested in you. If you're too obvious, it scares him away. You want to draw him in and you do this by playing it cool. This allows him to drop his guard so that he begins the hunt. It's pretty simple when you get right down to it.

It's like this: You go out on a date. You have a good time. You really like this guy. I mean, like, *really.* You go home. You wait. And wait. Then he doesn't call. Then you start wondering why and all that stuff and then… You start calling or texting him.

You can't do this. You just have to stop. Make a point to catch yourself when you're doing this and… Stop. The first time or two is the hardest to resist. After that, it does get easier.

Obsession is hard. It's hard to deal with because, well, it becomes the only thing in our minds, like a pop song we can't get out of our heads. One way to overcome it is to just think about other things. That's right. The best way to deal with obsession is just to stop thinking about it altogether. And then turn your attention to something else. Don't get hung up. Go back to work, check out some online shoe sales or whatever. Do what whatever it is that you have to do in order to get your mind off this guy. Just do it.

The gist is to just put him out of your mind by turning your attention to other things. Do whatever you have to do not to think about him and his lack of calling or texting you.

Also, if you find yourself wanting to go by places he is, or you might think he might be, stop. *Don't even go there.* At all. If you find yourself wanting to call, stop. Anything that you do that might make him wonder has to be stopped before its inception. And all you have to do is realize what you're doing and understand that if you continue you might just chase him away.

Think of it this way: Stop. Control. Think. First of all, stop obsessing about this guy. Then control the situation by doing something else, i.e. turning your mind to something besides this guy. And think about something else. You can do it but you *have* to do it. The point is to do it. This allows you to stop chasing and allows him to start chasing, which is more attuned to the natural order of things, don't you think?

And once you've got that under control, he might just call you. Funny how that works.

But, more importantly, you have to think of yourself as worth chasing. As I said earlier, you have to be of the opinion that if they don't want you, then you don't want them. You have to know that you are the prize, the treasure, the one he wants. And if he doesn't want you, there are plenty of other fish in that sea of men. I mean, there are a lot of other men out there.

Anyway. When you lower yourself to the point that you feel have to work for some guy, keep this in mind: If you and he do get together and decide to have children, you're the one who's going to have to get pregnant, as you are the female. He doesn't have to create a child in his belly. You do and that's a lot of hard work. Keep this in mind whenever you go out with someone new. This is the way

Mother Nature intended it. I believe she also intended for men to do the chasing and not the women.

I mean, if you look at it like this, why would a woman chase a man? He's just as interested in getting his genetics into the next generation as any woman is. You're actually doing him a big favor by even considering this. And I know most people probably don't think about this on a first date. However, your biology sure is, or at least your subconscious is doing this for you. That's something you don't have much control over.

It wouldn't hurt to take this factor into account on any new date. You need to size this guy up. You need to make sure that if you did get together he would come through in the end and help you raise a child. That's his job, after all. And it's his job to do the calling. So let him do it.

All I'm saying about that.

But, to reiterate, you have to do something that makes you seem like a prize and prizes are what you win when you work hard and compete. By just being a woman, you are the prize. He has to work hard for you to get you can you can be the prize he wins. Men are natural competitors and they like winning. Keep this in mind and allow him to do what he is predisposed to do and that is to chase after you.

HE'S NOT INTERESTED, RIGHT?

Even after it's all said and done, and even after he hasn't called or made so much as a peep in her general direction, some women will still wonder if this guy is interested in her or not. She might even go as far as to deny reality in order to get what she wants: For that damned man to answer her calls! She is willing to keep making a fool of herself because she wants to prove a point and no one is going to tell her this guy doesn't want her. She will stop at nothing to get his attention and once she does, she will keep at him until she wears him down and he just finally succumbs.

Yes, this kind of situation has happened. However, it never turns out well. Really, it doesn't and we don't have to go into detail about it, either.

However, if this is you, or someone you know, it can be hard to just accept the fact that a guy doesn't want you. It can turn you into a crazy person. It hurts but in order to avoid that hurt, these women simply don't accept the reality of the situation.

You just have to accept that he's not interested and you have to move on from that. If he doesn't call and if he suddenly starts avoiding you, it's because he's not interested. And it's possible he's not interested in you because he thought you were too interested. But in reality does it really matter? If he's not interested, you shouldn't be interested in him, either. The point is to never get hung up on a guy like this. Guys who act like this will always drive you crazy, even if you can manage to turn them into your boyfriend or whatever. And you'll always wonder about the sincerity of their love. Why keep at something just to prove a point? It's not worth the self-esteem you might lose in the end. So, if he doesn't show interest, it's usually best to nip it in the bud and move on because, in the end, moving on in a case like this is always the better option.

HOW TO MAKE HIM REALIZE HIS INTEREST

Keep in mind that men are going to be naturally interested in you because you are a woman. This is just the way it is. He's a man. You're a woman. That doesn't need much explaining, does it? So, yes, by the very virtue that you are a woman, he will be interested in you. It's just when that "something happens" that his interest wanes.

So, what went wrong? Why does the interest dry up? Who knows? But most likely it's because either you two didn't have that much in common or he somehow got put off. The point I want to make here, though, is to not worry about it too much. He's not interested, so who cares what really went wrong? Why worry about it?

I say, let go and move on. No man, in my opinion, is worth this much trouble. And, if you really think about it, you know that it's a lot of trouble and going to that much trouble just to prove someone is interested in us kinda sorta, defeats the purpose. Right? Right.

The other point to understand here is how to make him realize his interest in you. And that simply means, how to get him to start being curious about you. Yes, there has to be something there that sparks his interest. Who knows what that attribute is as it varies with different individuals. You can't really put a label or title on it. However, there is one thing that sparks a man's interest like no other and that is simply holding back. Yes, you do need to show a slight interest, like a smile or something so that he doesn't get completely discouraged. But, keep in mind that if you show him too much interest at first, he's going to be, well, disinterested. Men have trouble with this because it sparks a responsibility in them they might not be ready to deal with, especially if you two have just met. If it's all about you and your need to be with him, he's more than likely going to bail. And that's why he gets uninterested and doesn't want to call or text.

And that's why you have to accept this and move forward. It's very important to keep the upper hand and not come off as desperate. And needy. And we all know that desperate and needy aren't a good combination.

By holding back, you create demand and spark his interest. By the same token, if you act too desperate and bug him, it makes you look like you're not a valuable commodity. You're just the girl who's annoying him, the one who thinks he's so great that she can't live without him. This will boost his ego so much that he might begin to look for someone that is more "worthy" of his new found confidence, the confidence you inspired in him. In essence, you run the risk of creating a monster. If you fawn over him too much, he could become completely unbearable and might start thinking all women want him. This makes him want to find someone else, someone who will hold back and let him act like a man and start chasing. And then he'll be back in his place. And in the end, that's probably what they all want and more than likely what they need. Why not give it to them?

HE LOVES YOU? HE LOVES YOU NOT?

Before we go any further, I wanted to touch on this subject because it's important to know that not all guys who don't call or text are only a one-date phenomenon.

We've all had a guy that keeps popping up from time to time. Say you dated him in the past and, for whatever reason, it didn't work out. He's someone you probably liked a lot and couldn't get out of your head. You chased him a little and he gave you a little encouragement. For a while, you may have had something, even though he would never define what that something was. Were you in a relationship? *Maybe.* Were you dating? He didn't *think* so. Did you have a future together? Well, he never told you that. The two of you just sort of left that one hanging.

In effect, he gave you enough to keep you interested but then he always pulled away. He was the one who got away but was never really quite there.

But for some reason, this guy keeps popping up occasionally. Out of the blue he'll call you and want to meet or just talk. Maybe he wants sex or he's feeling lonely. Usually, he's between other women when he's doing this and wants something from you. You may even be on his roster of women. You may be one of many that he keeps around just in case. And now he's calling again.

This gets your head to reeling: What does he want? Does he like me now? Did he finally figure out he liked me and wants to make a go of it? Should I meet him? What might happen next?

Well, I always say, if you can't figure him out to begin with, then you're not going to do it now. I think these kinds of men just like stringing women along. And it's not just men that participate in this kind of behavior. Women do, too. They have a few guys on the side waiting just in case their first choice somehow falls through. This could be you. If it is, perhaps it's time to figure out why you do it. And the reason might just be because you like having options. That might be his reasoning too. Options are nice but when they toy with others' feelings, things can turn bad.

I say this: If you're not the first choice, why play the game at all? And whatever man is doing this to you should take you off his list completely. If you want to be his first choice, you have to demand that position. And you can't mind admitting that, either. This shows you have self-respect and self-respect is an invaluable asset. It shows you won't just fall at some man's feet and beg for attention. And why should you? You shouldn't. He should be working for your attention, not the other way around.

However, if you find that this happens to you, you have to make a firm decision about what you're going to do about him. I'm more than sure that you don't like not knowing where you stand with this guy. Maybe you do. People are different. Regardless, whatever your feelings, perhaps it's time to either go your separate ways or make him cue you in to what he's feeling.

Not knowing where you stand with a guy can make any girl crazy. So, I say, why not just ask him what your status is? Why not come right out with it and ask him, "Is this thing we have for real or is it not?" Or, even, "Do we have a relationship?"

This means you have to take a stand and let him know you won't stand for being lead on. I don't think it's ever a bad idea to set a guy straight by telling him you're not playing games anymore or you're no longer interested in just meeting him for a drink and, perhaps, some sex. If you don't want to meet him, then don't and if you don't want to engage in sex, then don't. It's up to you.

I know that this might be hard if you're feeling lonely yourself and need some male attention. However, if you do this, keep in mind that he's more than likely not going to be what you want in the end. He'll probably start playing those games again, giving non-committal answers and, generally, making you feel bad about yourself. I like to call it being wishy-washy. And who wants that? We wouldn't put up with it from friends, would we? No. And we shouldn't put up with it from a man, either.

I think the main culprit in this is the idea that because this guy never committed, he's a challenge to you. You want to win him over because he's left you with no closure. I mean, you didn't break up because you never really dated, right? And, therefore, there's no closure here and no closure means trying to figure out what this guy is after and what he's doing.

I'll tell you what he's doing. More than likely, he's just stringing you along. He's taking you for granted. He doesn't want to commit because he's not the type of guy who commits. He wants to keep his options open while having you as a back-up. If this isn't cool with you, why not ask him why he's doing this to you? What do you have to lose? It's always best to know his intentions right out of the gate. It's best to see whether or not you two match up with what you want out of the relationship. This way, you don't waste time on something that isn't going to happen and a relationship that is going nowhere. No one wants to waste time on something like this.

Also, see if there is a pattern with this guy and you know that if he contacts you, you will be powerless to control yourself, you might want to evaluate this. Essentially, if he is like your kryptonite and whenever he's around or contacts you, you lose all common sense and become so weakened in his presence, you merrily go along with him. The idea to get some perspective now before any of this happens, before you make a mistake with this guy.

In the end, I think it's sometimes best to just let sleeping dogs lie. Sometimes it's best not to stir the pot or disturb the mess. Maybe, in this case, it's best just to walk away from this one and move on to someone better. Just try not to put yourself in the situation to begin with just to get your hopes dashed again. Perhaps you could even block his calls so you can't receive them. Because, once he's got you hooked again, that's just more time wasted on this jerk which could be better spent finding another man who will more than likely treat you better.

You don't want this, this man who just pops in occasionally to get you confused again. You want a good man. A good man won't string you along like this. He won't make you wait on him. And he won't call when he just wants to get laid. So, let this one go if at all possible. He's trouble and will keep you on an indefinitely long leash. And that's not fun, especially when he's the one acting like a dog.

THE REAL REASON YOU WANT HIM

Why is it that these guys who don't call or ignore us make us want them like we want the latest "it" bag? What do they do that makes us so crazy we're willing to make complete fools out of ourselves over them? What do they have? Yeah, they're cute. Yeah, you could see yourself with them. Yeah, yeah and yeah. But what is it? What is it about these guys that turns us into hot messes? What do they do that makes us go out of our way for them?

They don't call, that's what they do. They leave us hanging. They ignore us. They leave us wanting more.

Well, that wasn't too much of a reach. But listen. This is why you want these guys and it's probably why you start calling them. He's not calling. There's radio silence. What's going on? Why can't I have him?

Get where this is going? When someone ignores you, sometimes our immediate reaction is to get them to *not* ignore us, even to the detriment of our self-esteem. We have to know why, why, why!

Why? Because he doesn't want to, that's why. He's not calling because he doesn't want to pursue a relationship.

And we can't stand that, can we? Nope. It's too hard to take. I mean, who wouldn't want to have a relationship with us? But… But what if… What if you look at it another way? What if you actually think about how the date really went? I'd almost be willing to bet that once you left him on that date or whatever, you were a bit ambivalent about him calling, weren't you? Were you like feeling like it would be okay if he calls but also okay if he didn't? But you knew, or at least you were sure that he would call. He was very interested in you, or so you thought. You figured that he had fallen for you and you were trying to figure out a way to let him down easy. But it didn't happen that way. You fully expected him to call or text but when he didn't, you started to wonder why he didn't want you. And that's what got you hooked.

Not knowing why someone doesn't want us makes us act in ways we would normally never act. But if you think of it in other ways, then it might be easier to take.

Take a job interview. You dress up, you look nice, you're affable and your interviewer seems to like you well enough. But then you don't hear anything. They did give you the standard, "You'll be hearing from us in one to two weeks." And so you wait on the call. Not only that, you know that you have no choice but to wait and you know that if they don't call, they passed. Right? And while this can suck and make you feel bad, you do get over it because it was just a job and you know with your qualifications that you will find something even better. And more importantly, you understand that this is just the way it is.

Why not look at a guy not calling the same way? You take the place of the person who's filling a spot. Take the "I won't call him; he'll call me" approach. And by this I mean, instead of thinking you should call him, why not just decide that if he's interested, he will call. And if he's not, he won't.

Yes, this may seem a bit impersonal. But what's wrong with that? Going on a date is sort of like going on a job interview and if you begin to view it as such, it will be easier to get through it. Yes, I understand that when someone doesn't respond to us, something inside of us gets triggered and we start going crazy. I don't think it's driven by lust or desire or even love a lot of times. I think it's because we can't stand to be ignored. Human don't like that very much. It drives us crazy.

Let's look at it this way. Say you've gone out on a date with some guy who really got on your nerves. When he said he'd call, you prayed he wouldn't. But he did call, didn't he? He called and called and drove you almost insane until you flat-out told him that you weren't interested and to stop calling. Am I right?

And now it's happening to you. This other guy you liked implied that he'd call and he didn't. And now you're in the place where the guy you didn't want to be with found himself in. You ignored him, he kept calling. Now, you're getting ignored and you can't stand it. It's perfectly understandable. But it's also important to get a grip right now so you don't chance making a fool out of yourself. In essence, the one you want is now out of your reach and that makes you want him like nothing else.

Now, hold that thought. Think about it. Do you get it? Being the girl who is out of reach is what every man wants. They want to be with that person who doesn't want them, who they can't have. It's crazy, isn't it? And why is that? Why do we want the ones who don't want us? Are we gluttons for punishment? Do we secretly hate ourselves? Are we masochists?

None of the above. We're human! This is how humans operate. And this is a very good insight into the male mind, I might add. This could be used to your advantage in the future.

Being the girl who is seen as a commodity, someone worth going for is like having a goal for a guy. Why do you think everyone wants a luxury car and a big house? For most, they are something worth working for. Therefore, they become a goal. And that's what drives us as humans—goals. We have to have goal, otherwise, what's the point? The idea is to get him to think of you as valuable and, hence, you become his goal.

And it's easy as one, two, three. I will cover all this in more detail in following chapters, but suffice it to say that if act like you don't want him, he'll probably want you more. And if you do this, you can hook him like a fish.

LET HIM CALL YOU

Want a clear-cut way of avoiding any closure issues after the date is said and done? What to know the best way to deflect responsibility in the "who's going to call whom" game? It's easy and so simple. All you have to do is simply tell him, "Call me."

That's right. When the date's over and you're starting to part ways, give him a nice smile and tell him to call you if he wants to do this again. That is, of course, if you actually want to go out again. If you don't like him, then just tell him it was nice and you'll see him later. Just never put yourself in the position where it looks like you're going to be the one doing the calling. Forget that. Let him do the legwork.

This is why I say that if you liked him and would like to see him again, give him a tad of encouragement. Hand it over to him, tell him to call you. You could even add, "You've got my number, right?" That way, you're not stuck wondering if you forgot to give him your number or whatever. You're not stuck wondering what to do. That way, you know that you said it and that he's also got your number. He knows you're interested without you falling all over yourself trying to convince him of your worth. You're putting it out there without waving a banner. And you're making sure he's got your number. This way, if he doesn't call that means he's not interested and you can get over it and move on with your life.

But don't wait on his call. Don't wait for him to call you and, of course, don't call him. And certainly don't text him.

The main idea behind this is that you have to stop waiting on a guy to call or text and you have to start living your life. Keep in mind that life is passing by as we speak. If you wait and wait on a guy to call, even one that might just be perfect, and he never does, you've just wasted a lot of time. Time that could be better spent finding someone who *will* call. This is about you living your life and not waiting. That's all. It's not a failure if he doesn't call. It just means you weren't meant to be together. That's all.

STOP THE WAITING GAME

Waiting on a man to call can be absolute torture. I think we've established that. But one of the main things to keep in mind while all of this is going on is make sure you have a full life. That way, you're not really waiting. You're just living your life, doing your own thing, having fun. It means you're not focused so much on him calling, but instead are focused on yourself and your life.

Not being so focused on waiting on a guy to call or text can help you in so many ways. It can alleviate some of the anxiety as well as bring your life, as you live it, into the forefront. What I mean by that is you think of other things besides him and his call. It takes some of the importance away from it. And it allows you to relax more.

So, if you keep yourself busy during the meantime, when he does call, you'll be more relaxed and not obsessed about him calling. And then you will be able to listen to what he's saying. This will help the excitement wear off a little so that you don't seem like a giddy school girl. And this will let him know that you haven't been waiting by the phone but instead have been out and about enjoying your life without him. This should make him wonder about you, about what kind of woman you are, and this will get him to thinking of you in a more positive light. He'll think you're a woman with a lot going on, things to do, and hey, look, you took the time to take his call. It will make him feel special.

And then he might just start thinking you're someone special, too. And that's what you're after.

How Long Should You Wait on His Call?

After your date, some might wonder how long you should wait between the date and the follow-up call. This can vary from guy to guy as many of them have watched too many movies or have been told many different things by too many different people about the proper call time. So, obviously, this will vary depending on each, individual guy.

But, in my opinion, a good rule of thumb is three to seven days. Of course, if this guy really likes you, he might call you that night. This has happened before and it could happen to you if you really hit it off with him. Or he might call the next day. But if he's playing it cool, and we all know that men love to do this, he'll think he'll make you wait a few days after, just to be sure you know he's a busy guy and has more important things going on. Like you care. However, if he wants to play this game, this is also the same attitude you should have as well. If he waits this long, then you should act as though you could not have cared less if he called or not. Be friendly but don't act like your prayers have been answered or anything.

Seriously, you have to look at it like this: It's fine if he calls. It's fine if he doesn't. Either way, you are okay. Adopting this attitude means that you take yourself out of the loop and start seeing yourself as an interested observer. That's right. Observe his behavior. Check out what he's doing or not doing. And then think about it. Because, maybe, just maybe, you might not care if you ever hear from this guy again. And, if you're honest with yourself, you might be glad he doesn't.

But if you like him and he does call, the best thing to do is pick up and be friendly, like you knew he was going to call all along. Let him take it from there. Let him make the plans and go along. But don't gush or say, "I'm so glad you called! I was waiting forever!" Even if you were, he doesn't need to know that.

Oh, and enjoy yourself. Dating should be fun, you know.

As for the guy who makes you wait, even if he takes a few days, be pleasant. Just remember that guys get a lot of bad advice in this regard so, if you want to, cut him a little slack in the beginning. Just don't let it become a habit. If he waits several days again, you might want to start thinking about your options. No one likes waiting and most men who pull this sort of thing aren't worth waiting for.

WOMEN WHO ARE SUCCESSFUL WITH MEN

This leads us up to our next subject matter and that is how to get back out there and get dating with the idea of eventually finding a good man. To start, let's take a look at women who seem to have no trouble attracting men. This is something to aspire to, to get you motivated to get out there and do the same.

We've all seen women who go through men like we go through lattes. For whatever reason, they always have a date and always have men who want to date them. They are successful with men—*very* successful. Men love them. But why? What do they have that some of us don't?

First of all, they're there to have a good time. There is no vibe of desperation at all. They're not in it to find a husband. At least not yet. They just want to meet new men and go out and have something to do on a Saturday night. They're just, in effect, dating.

And that's why men love them. These women know what to do and what not to talk about. They present themselves with real confidence and, more importantly, know what they want. They are themselves and are comfortable being themselves.

Another thing these women do is that they have no real expectations of a relationship. When they go out with a guy, it's just to go out. They're not expecting him to be anything more than a first date. They're just getting to know him and that's it, at least for now. They have a very cavalier approach to dating and men and they, simply, go with the flow.

Also, they don't pressure men to have kids or settle down or move in together, even after they're dating. (Of course, they never bring this up on the first few dates.) They don't talk about these things because they are confident enough to know that, in due time, the man will bring it up. And if he doesn't, then they're, as they cliché says, not on the same page. And that means they're not suited for each other. No biggie.

However, if they do bring it up and their men don't want the same things they do—marriage, kids, etc.—they don't have a nervous breakdown about it. These women are willing to let him go if the guy doesn't want the same things she does. Believe me, they're not waiting for him to call or text and they're not going to call or text him.

If you can take these few things and apply them to your dating experiences, you can, more than likely, be much more successful at dating. And it's not that hard. Just be in it for the fun. Be confident that things will work out the way you want them to without you having to control everything. I don't think you can look at dating as a task you need to do to get to what you really want, whether it's a long-term commitment or marriage or whatever. Dating isn't a job and shouldn't be seen as such. In a lot of cases, it's not even a stepping stone to marriage. It is what it is and what it is an afternoon or an evening a man and a woman share to see if they're compatible enough to move forward.

So, if you look at it like this and just take some of the pressure off yourself to impress and to perform, you can actually enjoy dating. Keep in mind that these women have confidence and if you can start being confident—mainly by believing in yourself and just being yourself—you can make these guy like you and by like, I mean really, really, really like you. Men love women who like themselves. They love women who are comfortable in their own skins. And that's not too hard to do, is it?

Therefore, when you go out, just don't have any high expectations of the date, even if you really like the guy. Just go with the flow and relax. Also, know what you want. If it's a night of hanky-panky, then that's your business. If it's for a deeper, committed relationship, that's okay, too. Just don't pressure your guy into any of this. Let him enjoy himself, too. And, of course, let him go if it doesn't work out. That means if he doesn't call, then he's not the one for you. And so, you move on until you find the one who is.

The gist is this: Just relax, have some good times, be yourself and see where the night takes you. This is called letting go of control and you might find that this can be a lot of fun and you'll be much more likely to get what you want.

Meeting Him

In order to date more confidently, you actually have to have interaction with men. This means, you might actually have to meet someone new or, even, check out someone with whom you are already acquainted and would like to get to know better. Also, think about dating sites, which are a great way to meet men. Whichever way you want to play it, it's good to know how to actually do it.

It's not that hard. Keep in mind that men want to meet women and, if they're available, men want to date women they already know. For them, dating women is like a genetic predisposition. They like them. They like women like *you*. Therefore, meeting men isn't that hard. Most of the time, if they are normal, they are always willing to talk to you. You can meet a guy on the subway or at the grocery store. You can meet him through a blind date or via an online dating service. He could already work in your office building. The point is that once you meet him, you have to ascertain if he's the one you want to make yours. And, if so, that's where this information comes in.

So, let's say, for all intents and purposes, that you've met the guy of your dreams. Or you've seen him from across a crowded room. How do you make that connection to let him know you're in the world? It's simple. You send him a signal. (I covered this in my book *Man Magnet*.)

A signal is nothing more than a casual glance and a slight smile. This lets him know you're there, in the world, and if he's game, he can come over to see what might happen. Obviously, don't start waving at him and beckoning him over. You have to be a bit more subtle.

Men are nature's natural aggressors, so it would stand to reason that he should be able to make the effort to come over to you and introduce himself. But what if he's shy? Then you might want to make the first move. This means you just smile at him and nod slightly, letting him know that you think he's cool and that you won't bite if he talks to you. Once you make that contact, he should come over. And once he does, all it takes is a simple "hello," and you're good to go.

That's it? Yes, that's it. I think dating is just making connections with others. It doesn't have to be too complicated. If you boil it down to the bare essentials, then you will find that the simpler applications are usually the best. Why make such a big fuss? Why not just say "hello" and see where it goes? This lets him know that's it's okay for him to approach and start a conversation. And that's where all great relationships begin.

But what if you send the signal and he doesn't come over? Then he's out of the equation and you have to find someone else. If he was a fish, then he just wasn't biting. You just have to let it go. This might sting a little and if so, feel the embarrassment and then let it go. There are plenty of men who will want to get to know you better, believe me. Never, ever get hung up on one guy. If he doesn't take the bait, be willing to let it go and move on. Getting hung up on one man or on a rejection is what keeps many women from finding the man of their dreams. You have to let things go.

Keep in mind that all men are different and some will be more aggressive than others. That's okay; just know that you might have to deal with these guys from time to time. If you come across one, and you don't like him, just make an excuse and leave. It's not worth ruining your night over.

The idea is to get out there and try out a few things and see what happens. I think going in with an open-mind is what works best. If you go in expecting to find the best man to ever have existed, you're more than likely going to be disappointed. However, if you go in thinking you'll meet a few guys here or there and have a good time, you will. It's not about lowering your expectations but putting them in alignment with reality. That's not what I'm saying. What I'm saying is to go in thinking you're just there to have fun and maybe meet a nice guy. That's all.

Let's move forward and say that you two have come together and now it's time to get to know him better. But, obviously, you need a conversation starter. That's no problem. Just introduce yourself, allow him to do the same, perhaps shake hands and then pull something out of the air, anything you like, even, "It's crowded in here, isn't it?" And let nature take its course.

Talking to men is easy. Just be willing to relax and let him talk, too. As you start to talk, compliment him on his nice outfit or whatever. Ask him about his work. Ask him what the time is. And say it with ease, with a disarming smile and allow him to respond. Once you ascertain whether or not you want to get to know him better, let nature take its course. You've just met him and that is the first step to start dating again.

REMEMBER: ABSENCE MAKES THE HEART GROW FONDER

One of the best pieces of advice that I've ever heard is this: Absence makes the heart grow fonder. And isn't that true? If you're shoved up against someone for hours at a time, on an airplane for instance, they're more than likely going to get on your nerves. If your mom calls you every single day, she begins to drive you crazy. If you have a neighbor who drops by your place every day wanting to borrow a cup of sugar and to gossip until the wee hours of the morning, she's going to get on your nerves. And what about that friend who wants to meet at the same place for lunch every day and talk/complain about the same things? Ugh!

You get the point.

So, would it not stand to reason that if a guy you like, and who quite possibly likes you, don't see one another for a few days, then both of you will feel better about one another? I think so. Being apart even for a few days at a time gives a person time to breathe and relax and to start thinking of another in an amorous way.

You have to give him space so that he will begin to miss you. If you're hanging around all the time, he'll never have the opportunity to miss you. By the same token, if you're all up in his face all the time or calling him constantly, he's not going to think of you as a potential girlfriend or whatever. He's just going to get irritated.

And you'd do the same thing, too. If some guy was badgering you about a date all the time, you'd probably go off on him, right? More than likely, yes.

So, I say, back off a little and let things just marinate. Let him think about you instead of just talking to you every day. He will start to become more attracted to you because he hasn't talked or seen you for a little while. You will become more of a mystery and someone he wants to get to know better. And that's what you're after. And all you have to do to get there is not call him and let him call you. And, sometimes, be busy when he calls. Pretty simple, isn't it?

You Want Him to Want You

Yes, we're going there. It's all about playing hard to get but with a caveat: Not playing *impossible* to get. It's not that hard to do, either. And if you can pull this off, men don't really have a choice in the matter. Playing hard, but not impossible to get, is the way women land men.

Once you meet a man, or even on your first date, it's important to know how to make him want you. And one good way of doing that is to play hard to get. Yes, we all know that if you play hard to get you have the potential of driving men insane with want. However, this is only sometimes true. It does drive them crazy and that *can* be fun to watch. However, you can't overplay your hand here. You have to strike a balance.

The general idea is this: You have to play hard to get but not so hard that you risk losing him. In effect: You can't be so unavailable or elusive that he loses interest. You have to give him a little to pique his interest but not the whole show. You have to let him know that you're interested but *not too interested*. If you can do this, you can get that man. The main ingredient to this is to spark his interest and get him hooked. You can do this in innumerable ways, but the main thing to do is simply act like a woman. That's it. Be a woman. Dress like a woman. Act like a woman. And let him see you as a woman. This allows him to be a man.

Obviously, this doesn't mean to go all slutty, either. That's not what this is about. No, you give it a little at a time, here and there. This could be by saying something flirty and dressing well, or possibly using your cleavage to your advantage. This just shows a man that you're a woman and men want women. When you do this, you also show him that you are available to him in that way. Maybe. Not now, but *maybe* in the future. Get what I'm saying? It's all about flirting and showing him that you're interested but not so interested right now.

But here's the rub: While you may appear available, you may not be. That means you're not giving anything away right now. Perhaps, at a later date. But not now. You're just showing him you are capable of such things. That's all. You're not doing anything right this instant.

This is how you pique his interest. This is how you make him want you. And you can do it fairly easily as it's something all women are more than capable of. The main idea behind this is to inspire the man to chase you, not literally, of course, but to strive to win you over. This means no calling him and no chasing him. This means leaving it all mostly up to him. Yes, you run the risk of him not chasing you, but then again, if he doesn't chase even a little, he's probably not interested at all.

Mostly, all of this is just acting like you're a little coy. You're not teasing him per se, but you're not *not* teasing him, either. The idea is to laugh softly at his jokes. Smile and then look away.

Also, when you get that first kiss, be sure to just kiss a little and then pull back. You can't give him the whole show the first night, after all. When you're eating dinner, actually eat your food; don't just push it around your plate. You don't have to chow down like a truck driver, but keep in mind that most men like women who eat. If you're standing, lean in towards him when you're talking so he will have to bend down to hear you. This creates immediate intimacy and he will like being that close to your body and that means he will probably want to see you again.

Keep in mind that when you do this, it has to be like you've always done it, like this is who you are. Practice in the mirror at home if you have to. Why not? Just be casual and be yourself. If you're nervous, just try to play it off until you feel more comfortable. Keep in mind that he's more than likely nervous about your date, too. So, relax and this will allow him to relax and then you can start to pique his interest and make him want you, which is sure to drive him crazy. Hey, it's okay. He'd do it to you if he could.

Make Him Work for It

Now, let's get to it. You've met him. You like him. He likes you. You've had your first conversation and he's called to ask you on a date. You've replied in the affirmative. Now what? After the date is said and done, you should know whether or not you want to keep this thing going and/or if you potentially want him to be your new boyfriend or not. If so, then it's time to do just that. If not, say bye-bye and move onto the next one.

However, if you think this guy is a possibility, let's figure out how to make him yours. Everyone wants what they can't have. Therefore, make him work for it.

I know this might sound a little harsh, but you have to basically treat men like they should be happy you're taking the time. If you do this, you won't appear to be love-struck by him and that means you are not putting yourself in a subservient position. In a way, it's almost like you're doing him a favor by going out with him.

Of course, a balance must be maintained. You can't act snooty and roll your eyes when a man asks you out. The gist is that you're a busy woman and he should be glad that you're willing to go out with him, not the other way around. This leads to you being in charge. And this is how it should work.

If you do this, it lets the man know that you won't take crap, nor will you be treated like crap. It means that he must show some respect. And if he can't do that? Then he's probably not worth the trouble. In effect, you make him work for it.

This might make some women a little nervous. *Him working to get me?* Yes, and if you think this way, then this is probably where a lot of insecurity is coming from. To think like this means that you don't think you're worth it and that you have to persuade a man to get him into a relationship. Nothing could be farther from the truth but you have to stand up and assert yourself. This means you have to believe in yourself enough to be willing to take the chance that he might walk if you don't fawn all over him. And if he does walk? Bye-bye.

You should never look at any one man as the end-all-be-all, especially if you're not dating them long-term or aren't already married to them. Until they've put a ring on your finger, they're just a guy you're with. And you have to look at it like that. Sure, you might be having fun or what-have-you, but until there is some displayed or spoken level of commitment, he could walk at any time.

So, in other words, without this level of commitment, where does that leave you? In limbo, that's where. And this is not a fun place to be. You don't want to be in limbo, but you wouldn't mind him thinking he's in limbo, would you? No, you wouldn't. Yes, this may seem a little hard-nosed, but if you don't do it, then you're left in a very precarious position. Who wants that? No one.

There are men out there who don't do much to get women. One of the reasons why is because women allow this to happen. It's okay if he doesn't buy dinner or okay if he's late. But, in my opinion, no, it's not. And to allow things like that to slide means you're allowing him to treat you however he likes. If you want to be wanted, and you want to make him yours, you can't be a doormat. It's *that* simple.

You have to put yourself in control. This means don't be at his beck and call. Whenever he calls, don't rush to the phone. Let it ring and call him back a little later. It's okay. He'll still be there. I know that in the first stages of a relationship it's hard not to want to talk and be with your man all the time. However, too much one-on-one can lead him to feeling hemmed-in. No man wants to feel like he's been captured.

If you can hold back a little and not act like you have nothing else going on but him, you can show him how valuable you and your time are. This puts you in the power position. Again: *This lets him know how valuable you are.* Using control in this way shows him that you have a lot going on and you are taking time out of your busy life to go out with him. He should be grateful and he should start to see the value in you and the potential of a future relationship. And this leads to you making him your boyfriend or whatever. And all it takes is making him work for it. Not that big of a deal, is it?

A Crucial Element

While this goes along with the previous chapter, I wanted to make sure that this element wasn't overlooked. Let's get to it.

Ah, you've finally met a good man and you want him like nothing else. He's oh, so cute! He's got a good job and… Ah, the fantasies are already starting to take over. It's you, him and your life together. It's going to be so great! It's going to be—

Stop. You can't do this to yourself. Over-fantasizing about a man is usually a one-way ticket to disappointment and resentment. It's fun; I'm not saying it isn't. But if you want him to like you like you like him, and, obviously, you do, there is something you can do that has the potential to seal the deal and make him yours. Ready for it?

You can't let him know how much you want him.

This is *the* crucial element in making a man want you, therefore, landing a good man and, therefore, making him yours. This is *the* thing that many women overlook when dating men. It's a biggie.

Let's reiterate.

A most important fact: You can't let him know how much you want him. If you let him know you want him *this* much, he's going to lose interest. But if you hold back and don't let him know how much you like him, he's going to wonder if you do.

Get it? This sparks interest and want in a man, not knowing how much a woman wants him. He'll be wondering, *Does she or does she not she like me?* And when he starts wondering that, he's more than likely going to get hooked.

This is the most important thing I can tell you and with this, I say to use with caution and at your discretion. This was the main element in my book, *How to Be Wanted*. It's how to make a man want you and want you badly.

The main reason many women don't utilize this is because they are afraid of losing their men. Hey, it's a legitimate fear. However, if this is the case that means they are probably sending out signals of desperation and this makes a man want to escape more than anything else.

However, if you can get over the desperation factor and use the idea of concealing your true desire to your benefit, you can, more than likely, seal the deal. And all you have to do is not let him know how much you want him. And, let's face facts, if he's a hottie, you want him and you want him badly. However, to fall at his feet might just seal your doom. Who wants that? Don't you want to be in control? I don't see why not. If you do this, you can't fall all over him all the time and blow smoke up his butt about how great he is. Sure, you can tell him you like his shirt or that he looks good, but you shouldn't overdo it. Right now, in this first stage of what our ancestors called "courting" he's supposed to be wooing you. He's supposed to be chasing you. But what if he's not? He's not much of a catch, is he? Nope. Face the facts. You want a good man, not one with an ego so huge you have to console or feed it at all times.

And don't you deserve to be chased? Sure, you do. And all you have to do is to keep in mind that the less he thinks you want him, the more he will want you.

Yes, in a way it does sound counterintuitive. But it works and it works because men don't like things to be easy. If you've been in relationships before, you know this. If something is too easy, or, say for instance, a woman is too easy, then there is something off with that whole situation. It's like asking for directions. Men hate to do this, even though it would be easier than driving around for hours guessing where some place is. But they can't see it because they have to prove that they can find it on their own. It's the same thing. While it would be easier to just ask for directions, it's hard for them to do so. But try telling that to a man. He's just going to ignore it. The same principal applies here. If you're too easy for him, he's probably just going to ignore you, too.

To use an odd analogy, it's like giving a dog a treat. If you just hand it to him, he'll take it and then walk off and eat it. But if you hold it up out of his reach, he wants it more badly than he did before. It's that simple. Give a dog a bone and he likes it. Make a dog work for it, he *loves* it.

By the way, I'm not saying men are dogs. Well, at least most of them aren't anyway. It's just an analogy.

The gist is this: If you want him, you have to act as though you don't want him or that you could take him or leave him. Either way is okay. This keeps you at a slight distance, just out of reach. This gives you an advantage. This means you're not acting desperate and you're not coming on too strong. You're the girl who's playing it cool, which makes you cool to be around because she's not putting any pressure on him. You're not talking marriage and babies, you're just having fun.

And, really, it's supposed to be fun. Dating should be fun! Finding the man of your dreams should be a fun process. It's putting desperation into it and holding a ticking biological clock like a time bomb that takes all the fun out. If you back it down a little, you can see it for the fun times it's supposed to be. This means you're letting your relationship evolve at its own pace.

Men like a girl who has a little mystery. It makes them curious to find out more about you. If you do that, he'll want to figure you out. If you become a mystery to him, you have the potential to hook him and hook him in major way. All you're doing is leaving him wanting more.

Doesn't that sound like fun? Keeping him guessing means instilling want in him and once he starts to want you, he will usually fall and fall hard. Then *he* can seal the deal. And all you have to do was hold back a little. This means don't tell him everything about yourself. This means not falling all over yourself for him. He won't appreciate that. It might just scare him off. All you're doing is keeping him guessing whether or not you like him. This makes the wheels in his mind turn and try to figure you out. It's really that simple. Sure, be nice, be affable, but don't gush over him.

Why is this such a crucial element anyway? Well, the main reason is probably because men don't like to feel trapped. They want to be in charge. If you come on too strong, he'll feel a little overwhelmed and might just scurry off. But if you relax and let him come to his own conclusions, then he might just come to you.

Worth trying? If so, use with caution because once you hook him, he's probably gonna stay hooked. Only use this with someone you really want to make yours.

Also, keep in mind that you can't overdo this or he might think you're not interested at all. There is a fine line that exists between snubbing someone and actually taking an interest in them. So, be nice and receptive but not too much. The gist is, as always, to just leave him wanting more and that means sometimes playing a little hard to get. It's more like you're putting him into your schedule, not the other way around.

SLIGHTLY INTERESTED

One of the biggest things you can do is to not show too much interest. If you're overly enthusiastic about everything he says, he might wonder what's going on with you. *Why is she so interested in everything? I'm not that funny.* Remember, men like an air of mystery about how you feel and if you gush over him, he'll know how much you like him right off the bat. That might be good in the fact that it lets him know you're into him. It might be bad in the fact that he might not have made his mind up about being so interested in you.

So, all you have to do is hold back a little at first. Listen to what he's saying and nod and interject when necessary. Sure, ask him questions about himself and allow him to do the same. But if you can hold back a little and not try to find out every single thing about him, he might want to eventually find out everything about you.

See how this works? It's not that hard to figure out but if you can act only slightly interested and leave him wanting to know more about you, then you might just get yourself a new man.

You see, if you do this, you're letting him know that you want him and you're willing to step this thing you two have in this moment up to the next level. And, as previously discussed, he might not be ready for that. Therefore, it stands to reason that if you're too interested in him, he might want to run, right?

Why do men do this? I think it's because if they go along in that moment, it will be harder later on to break up with you if he figures out he doesn't want a long-term commitment. He's simply avoiding later pain. He might be lazy, too, and not want to get committed to do something that is going to cause him to have to *do something*, which means he isn't worth having.

And it stands to reason, right? Most women have done this with men, too. We meet a guy and he's really into us. We can tell that he wants us. But, more often than not, that just makes us want to avoid him because we think, "If I let him think I like him, he will want more and I am not ready for more."

On the flip side of this, if the men we meet and date don't give us everything at first and don't show us that much interest, we get interested in them, right? Sometimes *overly* interested. We think, *How can he not be interested in me?* And that leads us to acting needy and opens us up to being his doormat.

In a way, this is simply surrendering control of the situation. It's allowing whatever happens to happen without you pulling and prodding and trying to manipulate it. Of course, this doesn't mean you need to be an ice queen, either. No. You can be affable and nice without being gushing. A balance must be attained and once you attain it, it will come like second nature. Stay inside your comfort zone but be willing to hold back when necessary and also to show interest when appropriate. It's mainly important that you don't go overboard with too much interest in him.

So, all you have to do is play it cool. Never show him how much you really like him. Let him do the talking. Keep in mind, that you've just met this guy or that this is your first date. Yes, you really might like him but you don't know if it's going to work out or not. Neither does he. You're in the primary stages. Take the time to feel the situation out. And let him do the same. This is called breathing room, so give him some of that. And then see where it goes and let nature take its course. If it ends up being a dud of a night, then so be it. Just move on to the next guy. Soon enough you will find one that you really click with and that's what you're really after, finding a man that's good and good for you. What better thing is there?

DON'T TRY TOO HARD

Another thing to remember when trying to find a good man is this: Don't try too hard. That's right. The harder you try, the less likely your man will want to become yours. This is true of most things. The more you try to do something, the less likely it is to happen. Have you ever noticed this? I have and it's seems to be especially true when dealing with men. If you try too hard with men they always seem to back off. I mean, if you start baking him cookies and showing up at his ballgames or whatever, most of the time he will start to withdraw. But if you hold back a little, you allow the mystery of "Where is she?" or "What's she's doing?" or even, "When will I see her again?" start to swim inside his mind. He will think of you when you're not there and when that happens, you've got him hooked. Which is the point, right?

You should keep in mind that the more they think you want them, the less they want you. It's unbelievable, but this is usually the way it is. Since this is the case, why not turn the tables on them? Act disinterested. Shrug your shoulders. Smile but don't let the conservation linger. Every once in a while, act like you have someplace better to be. In essence, you have to keep him guessing. Keep in mind that when it comes to men, it pay to be nonchalant.

Now this may sound like you're playing games, but it's better to play than to sit on the sidelines, isn't it? If you don't play the game, it will play you. I've seen it happen a million times.

However, you can't force anything into action just like you can't force some guy into liking you. If you do that, if you push something, it usually has the opposite effect and peters out on its own. Sad but true.

What to do? Stop trying so hard. What's the alternative? Keep it up and continue to fail? Why not just stop trying so hard and let things naturally evolve on their own? When you let go in this way, you are releasing and releasing is a good thing. You're letting go of what you thought worked and you're trying something new. However, you're not putting that much effort into it. It seems like a win-win to me. And how are you releasing? You're letting go of any preconceived outcome when it comes to any guy you meet. He might not be the love of your life, you know? He could just be some guy you saw for a while. Treat them all as such and maybe eventually see them eating out of the palm of your hand.

Taking this attitude is a good way to let these guys know you're valuable. And also, to help you take your power back. Always remember that you are a prize and you are worth making a big deal over.

No Need to Be Desperate

By not trying so hard, we are giving up on a needy, desperate attitude. If you have this, you will turn off every guy you meet because men do seem to run from anyone they think might want to pin them down. That's just the way it is. So, do the same thing with him, even if you are in total lust.

Man can smell desperation on woman and when they do, they usually hit the bricks. But sometimes it's just inevitable that we get desperate to date someone we really desire. That's human nature and shouldn't be looked down upon. It's a fact of life. It may be true that you might actually feel desperate but you can't show it. You will only achieve the opposite of what you want.

The only way to get over being desperate is to get a positive, confident attitude. You can do this by being more positive in your life and by letting go of any old grudges. Also, getting over any old hurts can help you feel so much better. When we replay things that hurt us in our pasts, we are simply feeling sorry for ourselves and that can be a big bummer. It's hard to be happy and positive when all one thinks about is all the wrongs that have happened to them over the years. And it's hard to meet a really good guy if you're carrying all this negative baggage around, too.

If you can get past all the things like this that may be holding you back, you can take the desperate out of dating and really start to move forward. It's just getting into that mindset that you are worth it; you are worth having a guy make a big deal out of you and you deserve happiness. That's the attitude you need, so say to yourself, even if you don't feel it, "I deserve happiness." Because you do. We all do.

In time, as you get more comfortable with yourself and landing men you really want to date, the desperation will go away.

A Bad First Impression

It is very important that when you introduce yourself to anyone, that you do so with confidence and a smile. This lets the world know that you are secure with yourself and you have self-confidence. This is a good way to be on a date, too, as it lets him know from the get-go that you are comfortable with yourself and probably won't put up with a lot of nonsense.

Sometimes, though, it's hard to make a good first impression. We get tongue-tied and then we use self-deprecating humor to disarm those we're being introduced to. This is all well and good if it comes off right; however, it's pretty easy to mess up and can come off badly and only serve to convince your date of your bad qualities. This always makes a bad impression. And a bad first impression might just equal no call and no second date.

The bit of advice here is to just introduce yourself, shake hands and smile. I wouldn't advise trying to put on airs or making a joke right off the bat, even if you're joking about yourself. When you just act like the person you are, you tell the world you're confident in yourself and have no need to be anyone you're not. You also tell the world, and your date, that you like yourself and that might just make him like you even more.

People like people who like themselves. This lets them know that you're not trying to get anything out of them but instead are offering them a peek into your world. People are curious about other people. They always have been and always will be. This means he will be interested in you just by the fact that he wants to go out on a date or that he's talking to you at a social event. So, you're already ahead and there's no need to over-impress. Besides, I say let him impress you.

Self-deprecating humor can work, but you have to be careful. It has to be in context and can't be too deprecating. So, making fun of yourself is probably not a good idea. However, if you trip and fall against him right when you meet, it won't hurt to poke fun of yourself a little: "Oh, klutzy me! Sorry!" And then laugh a little. Hey, stuff happens and playing it off like that ain't a bad way to start the evening. But keep in mind here that the idea is to be easygoing and nice. That's all. It means to give a good first impression without over-ingratiating yourself. Smile, be affable and let him do all the heavy lifting. Remember, though, to always leave him wanting more but don't be so hard to get he thinks you're uninterested.

You can show him you're slightly interested, as we talked about before, by simply touching his arm and or smiling at his jokes. Let him know it's okay for him to continue with you. But don't overdo it. Don't gush over him or show too much interest. This shows him you're mature and gives off an air of sophistication and it will usually leave him with a good first impression of you, which should spark his interest more than enough to warrant a call.

Making a good first impression can sometimes be a little tricky, so, if it takes you a few times to ease into this, that's okay. Just take your time and if you flub it up, laugh it off. Remember, dating is supposed to be pleasurable and finding yourself a good man shouldn't be hard work. Keep it light and easy and without any heavy expectation of what's to come or what might happen with this new guy. Once you can strike that balance, you should have him hooked. And getting one on the line is a very good feeling indeed.

In Conclusion

Sometimes, things happen that aren't exactly to our liking and instead of just accepting them, we try bending the world—or even a guy—to our will. Sad, but true. Sometimes a girl meets a guy who she really, really likes. They have a shared moment she thought was more than it was. Then he doesn't call her. And it sucks. And... Well, we all know what happens if she calls.

However, if she can take a step back and reevaluate the situation, she might just see where things went a little pear-shaped. And from that, she can pull herself up and get back out there and find a good man, a man who's willing to put in some time and effort to please her. Wouldn't that be fun?

Men aren't that hard to figure out. It's usually our reaction to *what men do* that gets things all screwy. When he doesn't call, we start blaming ourselves and become desperate. It doesn't have to be like this. All it takes is the ability to say no when the overwhelming desire to contact him comes calling. It also takes the ability to just let the guy be the man and do what he said he was going to do—call, text or show up or whatever. It's being willing to stop getting played, to stop feeling like a doormat and to get some confidence in order to move onto something better.

Dating should be fun and it shouldn't mean any more than what it is. And it's just two people getting together to see if they want to pursue a relationship. Or, maybe, it's just two people getting together to just do something fun, with no expectations. Make dating what you want it to be and then go for it. Why not just have some fun?

If you put the time and effort in, you can get back out there after a disappointing start, i.e. getting over some jerk not calling. And then you can get to dating and having so much fun. And then, perhaps, you can find a good man, a man that makes everything just a little more exciting and pleasing. And then you can make that man yours and not have to ever worry about some other jerk not calling again. And that, my friend, is a good feeling.

Good luck. I think our work here is done.

www.ingramcontent.com/pod-product-compliance
Lightning Source LLC
Chambersburg PA
CBHW022339280326
41934CB00006B/704